Workshop on Multilingual Language Resources and Interoperability 2006

(MLRI 06)

Held in conjunction with COLING/ACL 2006

Sydney, Australia
23 July 2006

ISBN: 978-1-61738-503-2

Printed from e-media with permission by:

Curran Associates, Inc.
57 Morehouse Lane
Red Hook, NY 12571
www.proceedings.com

Some format issues inherent in the e-media version may also appear in this print version.

Printed by Curran Associates, Inc. (2010)

Association for Computational Linguistics
209 N. Eighth Street
Stroudsburg, Pennsylvania 18360

Phone: 1-570-476-8006
Fax: 1-570-476-0860

acl@aclweb.org

Table of Contents

Preface

In an ever-expanding information society, many language processing systems are now facing the "multilingual challenge". Language resources, such as dictionaries, thesauri and wordnets, ontologies etc., as well as annotated corpora play an important role for the development, deployment, maintenance and exploitation of language processing systems.

Much work on architectures for multilingual language resources, on recommendations of best practice for creating, representing, maintaining and upscaling such resources has been done in the 1990s, but since then, most efforts in this field have had less visibility. On the other hand, much research and development work has been done on techniques for acquisition of language data, on upper ontologies, on resource standardisation, and, last but not least, on the Semantic Web.

One of the aims of this workshop it to provide an up-to-date view on issues relating to multilingual language resources and interoperability, in terms of language description, of technology and of applications. The development and management of multilingual language resources is a long-term activity in which collaboration among researchers is essential. We hope that this workshop will gather many researchers involved in such developments and will give them the opportunity to discuss, exchange, compare their approaches and strengthen their collaborations in the field.

The impressive overall quality of the submissions (22) made the selection process quite difficult but we would like to acknowledge the dedication of our program committee who provided many useful comments to all papers. During the reviewing process we took the decision to accept only 9 papers (about 41%) in order to allow for more discussions during the workshop.

The papers address a broad range of issues related with language resources for multilingual NLP applications, covering lexicons for general and specialised language, parallel corpora, and the acquisition of data from corpora.

In particular, questions of lexical modelling and of standards for lexical resources, as well as approaches to interoperability and resource sharing in a distributed infrastructure are in focus. As multiwords are an important part of any practically usable lexical resource, two papers have been selected which deal with questions of the representation and the corpus-based acquisition of multiword items (here: collocations), from a multilingual perspective. Finally, techniques for detecting parallel texts (here: English/Japanese) and a new view on the Bible as a truly multi-lingual resource for cross-linguistic information retrieval will be discussed as examples of approaches to get access to new sources of data for the creation of language resources.

Thus, the workshop covers central aspects of resource-related research; it is structured in a way to go upstream from lexicon standardisation and sharing, over lexical modelling to the identification and the use of corpora as a source of lexical data.

The organisation of this workshop would have been impossible without the hard work of the program committee who managed to provide accurate reviews on time, on a rather tight schedule. We would also like to thank the COLING/ACL 2006 organising committee who made this workshop possible. Finally, we hope that this workshop will lead to fruitful results for all participants.

Andreas Witt, Gilles Sérasset, Susan Armstrong, Jim Breen, Ulrich Heid, Felix Sasaki

Organizers

Chairs:

Susan Armstrong, ISSCO, Université de Genève, Switzerland
Jim Breen, Monash University, Australia
Ulrich Heid, IMS-CL, University of Stuttgart, Germany
Felix Sasaki, World Wide Web Consortium (Keio Research Institute at SFC), Japan
Gilles Sérasset, GETA CLIPS-IMAG, Université Joseph Fourier, France
Andreas Witt, Bielefeld University/Eberhard-Karls-Universität Tübingen, Germany

Program Committee:

Helen Aristar-Dry, The Linguist List
Susan Armstrong, ISSCO, Université de Genève, Switzerland
Pushpak Battacharya, IIT, Mumbai, India
Christian Boitet, GETA CLIPS-IMAG, Université Joseph Fourier, France
Pierrette Bouillon, ISSCO, Université de Genève, Switzerland
Jim Breen, Monash University, Australia
Nicoletta Calzolari, CNR, Pisa, Italy
Jean Carletta, University of Edinburgh, UK
Dan Cristea, University of Iasi, Romania
Patrick Drouin, OLST, University of Montreal, Canada
Scott Farrar, University of Arizona, Tucson, USA
Ulrich Heid, IMS-CL, University of Stuttgart, Germany
Erhard Hinrichs, Eberhard-Karls-Universität Tübingen, Germany
Claus Huitfeldt, Bergen University, Norway
Phanh Huy Khan, DATIC, University of Danang, Vietnam
Nancy Ide, Vassar University, Poughkeepsie, NY, USA
Kyo Kageura, University of Tokyo, Tokyo, Japan
Chuah Choy Kim, USM, Penang, Malaisie
Anke Lüdeling, HU Berlin, Germany
Mathieu Mangeot, Université de Savoie, France
Dieter Metzing, Bielefeld University, Germany
Massimo Poesio, University of Essex, UK
Alain Polguère, OLST, University of Montreal,Canada
Andrei Popescu-belis, ISSCO, Université de Genève, Switzerland
Goutam Kumar Saha, Centre for Development of Advanced Computing, CDAC, Kolkata, India
Felix Sasaki, World Wide Web Consortium (Keio Research Institute at SFC), Japan
Thomas Schmidt, ICSI, Berkeley, USA
Gilles Sérasset, GETA CLIPS-IMAG, Université Joseph Fourier, France
Gary Simons, SIL International, USA
Virach Sornlertlamvanich, Thai Computational Linguistics Laboratory, NICT, Thailand
C.M. Sperberg-McQueen, MIT Boston and W3C, USA
Manfred Stede, Potsdam University, Germany

Koichi Takeuchi, Okayama University, Japan
Dan Tufis RACAI, Uni Bucharest, Romania
Jun'ichi Tsujii, University of Tokyo, Japan
Takehito Utsuro, Kyoto University, Japan
Andreas Witt, Bielefeld University/Eberhard-Karls-Universität Tübingen, Germany
Michael Zock, LIF-CNRS, Marseille, France

Additional Reviewer:

Laurent Besacier, GEOD CLIPS-IMAG, Université Joseph Fourier, France

Workshop Program

Sunday, 23 July 2006

8:45–9:00 Registration

9:10–9:20 Opening Remarks

9:20–9:55 *Lexical Markup Framework (LMF) for NLP Multilingual Resources*
Gil Francopoulo, Nuria Bel, Monte George, Nicoletta Calzolari, Monica Monachini, Mandy Pet and Claudia Soria

9:55–10:30 *The Role of Lexical Resources in CJK Natural Language Processing*
Jack Halpern

10:30–11:00 Coffee break

11:00–11:35 *Towards Agent-based Cross-Lingual Interoperability of Distributed Lexical Resources*
Claudia Soria, Maurizio Tesconi, Andrea Marchetti, Francesca Bertagna, Monica Monachini, Chu-Ren Huang and Nicoletta Calzolari

11:35–12:10 *The LexALP Information System: Term Bank and Corpus for Multilingual Legal Terminology Consolidated*
Verena Lyding, Elena Chiocchetti, Gilles Sérasset and Francis Brunet-Manquat

12:10–13:45 Lunch break

13:45–14:20 *The Development of a Multilingual Collocation Dictionary*
Sylviane Cardey, Rosita Chan and Peter Greenfield

14:20–14:55 *Multilingual Collocation Extraction: Issues and Solutions*
Violeta Seretan and Eric Wehrli

14:55–15:30 *Structural Properties of Lexical Systems: Monolingual and Multilingual Perspectives*
Alain Polguère

15:30–16:00 Coffee break

16:00–16:35 *A Fast and Accurate Method for Detecting English-Japanese Parallel Texts*
Ken'ichi Fukushima, Kenjiro Taura and Takashi Chikayama

16:35–17:10 *Evaluation of the Bible as a Resource for Cross-Language Information Retrieval*
Peter A. Chew, Steve J. Verzi, Travis L. Bauer and Jonathan T. McClain

17:10–17:30 Closing remarks

LEXICAL MARKUP FRAMEWORK (LMF)

FOR NLP MULTILINGUAL RESOURCES

Gil Francopoulo[1], Nuria Bel[2], Monte George[3], Nicoletta Calzolari[4], Monica Monachini[5], Mandy Pet[6], Claudia Soria[7]

[1]INRIA-Loria: gil.francopoulo@wanadoo.fr
[2]UPF: nuria.bel@upf.edu
[3]ANSI: dracalpha@earthlink.net
[4]CNR-ILC: glottolo@ilc.cnr.it
[5]CNR-ILC: monica.monachini@ilc.cnr.it
[6]MITRE: mpet@mitre.org
[7]CNR-ILC: claudia.soria@ilc.cnr.it

Abstract

Optimizing the production, maintenance and extension of lexical resources is one the crucial aspects impacting Natural Language Processing (NLP). A second aspect involves optimizing the process leading to their integration in applications. With this respect, we believe that the production of a consensual specification on multilingual lexicons can be a useful aid for the various NLP actors. Within ISO, one purpose of LMF (ISO-24613) is to define a standard for lexicons that covers multilingual data.

1 Introduction

Lexical Markup Framework (LMF) is a model that provides a common standardized framework for the construction of Natural Language Processing (NLP) lexicons. The goals of LMF are to provide a common model for the creation and use of lexical resources, to manage the exchange of data between and among these resources, and to enable the merging of a large number of individual electronic resources to form extensive global electronic resources.

Types of individual instantiations of LMF can include monolingual, bilingual or multilingual lexical resources. The same specifications are to be used for both small and large lexicons. The descriptions range from morphology, syntax, semantic to translation information organized as different extensions of an obligatory core package. The model is being developed to cover all natural languages. The range of targeted NLP applications is not restricted. LMF is also used to model machine readable dictionaries (MRD), which are not within the scope of this paper.

2 History and current context

In the past, this subject has been studied and developed by a series of projects like GENELEX [Antoni-Lay], EAGLES, MULTEXT, PAROLE, SIMPLE, ISLE and MILE [Bertagna]. More recently within ISO[1] the standard for terminology management has been successfully elaborated by the sub-committee three of ISO-TC37 and published under the name "Terminology Markup Framework" (TMF) with the ISO-16642 reference. Afterwards, the ISO-TC37 National delegations decided to address standards dedicated to NLP. These standards are currently elaborated as high level specifications and deal with word segmentation (ISO 24614), annotations (ISO 24611, 24612 and 24615), feature structures (ISO 24610), and lexicons (ISO 24613) with this latest one being the focus of the current paper. These standards are based on low level specifications dedicated to constants, namely data categories (revision of ISO 12620), language codes (ISO 639), script codes (ISO 15924), country codes (ISO 3166), dates (ISO 8601) and Unicode (ISO 10646).

This work is in progress. The two level organization will form a coherent family of standards with the following simple rules:

1) the **low level specifications** provide standardized constants;

[1] www.iso.org

Proceedings of the Workshop on Multilingual Language Resources and Interoperability, pages 1–8,
Sydney, July 2006.

2) the **high level specifications** provide structural elements that are adorned by the standardized constants.

3 Scope and challenges

The task of designing a lexicon model that satisfies every user is not an easy task. But all the efforts are directed to elaborate a proposal that fits the major needs of most existing models.

In order to summarise the objectives, let's see what is in the scope and what is not.

LMF addresses the following difficult challenges:

- Represent words in languages where multiple orthographies (native scripts or transliterations) are possible, e.g. some Asian languages.
- Represent explicitly (i.e. in extension) the morphology of languages where a description of all inflected forms (from a list of lemmatised forms) is manageable, e.g. English.
- Represent the morphology of languages where a description in extension of all inflected forms is not manageable (e.g. Hungarian). In this case, representation in intension is the only manageable issue.
- Easily associate written forms and spoken forms for all languages.
- Represent complex agglutinating compound words like in German.
- Represent fixed, semi-fixed and flexible multiword expressions.
- Represent specific syntactic behaviors, as in the Eagles recommendations.
- Allow complex argument mapping between syntax and semantic descriptions, as in the Eagles recommendations.
- Allow a semantic organisation based on SynSets (like in WordNet) or on semantic predicates (like in FrameNet).
- Represent large scale multilingual resources based on interlingual pivots or on transfer linking.

LMF does not address the following topics:

- General sentence grammar of a language
- World knowledge representation

In other words, LMF is mainly focused on the linguistic representation of lexical information.

4 Key standards used by LMF

LMF utilizes Unicode in order to represent the orthographies used in lexical entries regardless of language.

Linguistic constants, like /feminine/ or /transitive/, are not defined within LMF but are specified in the Data Category Registry (DCR) that is maintained as a global resource by ISO TC37 in compliance with ISO/IEC 11179-3:2003.

The LMF specification complies with the modeling principles of Unified Modeling Language (UML) as defined by OMG[2] [Rumbaugh 2004]. A model is specified by a UML class diagram within a UML package: the class name is not underlined in the diagrams. The various examples of word description are represented by UML instance diagrams: the class name is underlined.

5 Structure and core package

LMF is comprised of two components:

1) **The core package** consists of a structural skeleton that describes the basic hierarchy of information in a lexical entry.

2) **Extensions to the core package** are expressed in a framework that describes the reuse of the core components in conjunction with additional components required for the description of the contents of a specific lexical resource.

In the core package, the class called *Database* represents the entire resource and is a container for one or more lexicons. The *Lexicon* class is the container for all the lexical entries of the same language within the database. The *Lexicon Information* class contains administrative information and other general attributes. The *Lexical Entry* class is a container for managing the top level language components. As a consequence, the number of representatives of single words, multi-word expressions and affixes of the lexicon is equal to the number of lexical entries in a given lexicon. The *Form* and *Sense* classes are parts of the *Lexical Entry*. Form consists of a text string that represents the word. Sense specifies or identifies the meaning and context of the related form. Therefore, the *Lexical Entry* manages the relationship between sets of related forms and their senses. If there is more than one orthogra-

[2] www.omg.org

phy for the word form (e.g. transliteration) the *Form* class may be associated with one to many *Representation Frames*, each of which contains a specific orthography and one to many data categories that describe the attributes of that orthography.

The core package classes are linked by the relations as defined in the following UML class diagram:

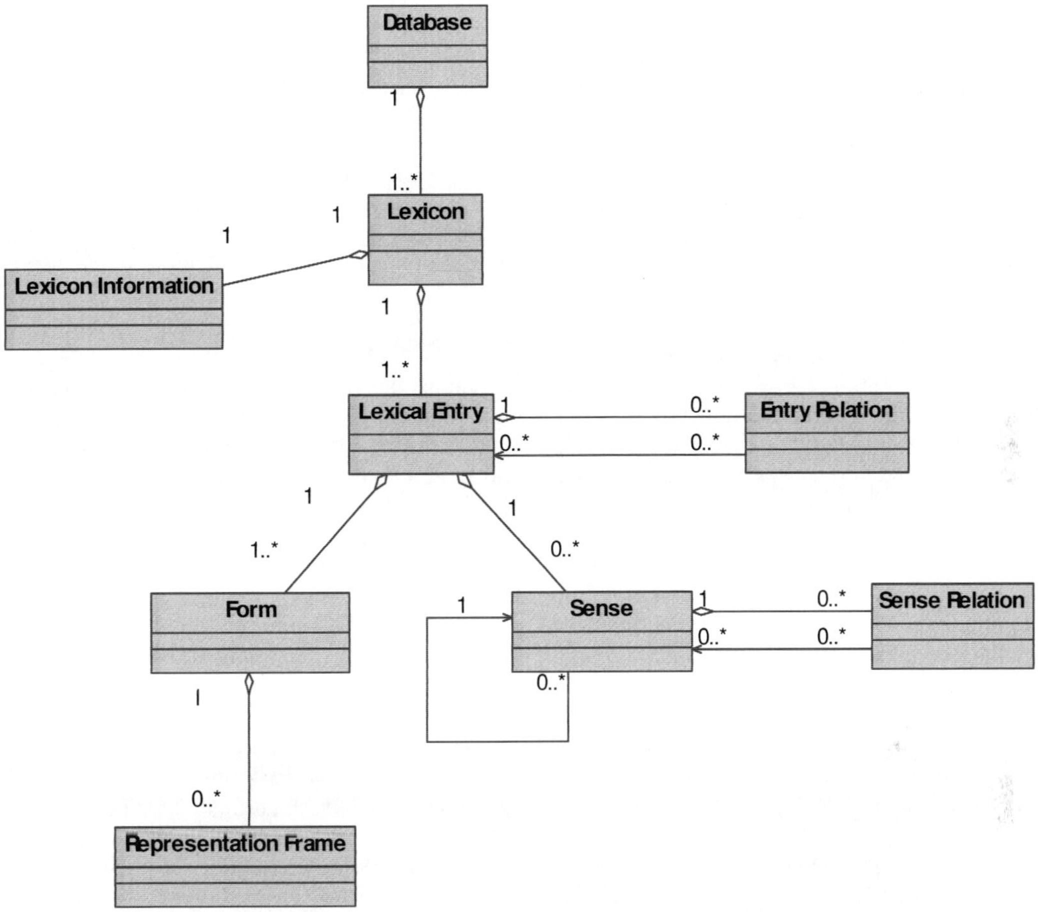

Form class can be sub-classed into *Lemmatised Form* and *Inflected Form* class as follows:

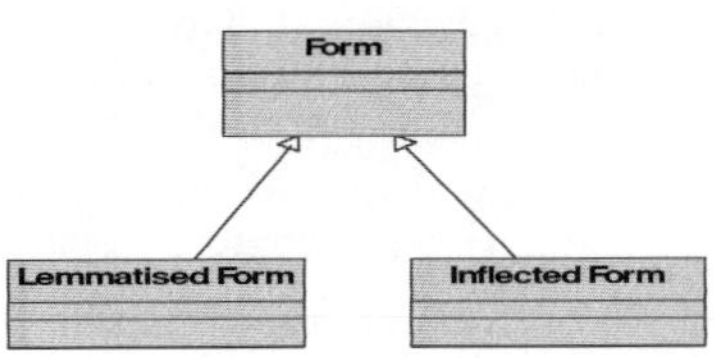

A subset of the core package classes are extended to cover different kinds of linguistic data. All extensions conform to the LMF core package and cannot be used to represent lexical data independently of the core package. From the point of view of UML, an extension is a UML package. Current extensions for NLP dictionaries are: NLP Morphology[3], NLP inflectional paradigm, NLP Multiword Expression pattern, NLP Syntax, NLP Semantic and Multilingual notations, which is the focus of this paper.

6 NLP Multilingual Extension

The NLP multilingual notation extension is dedicated to the description of the mapping between two or more languages in a LMF database. The model is based on the notion of Axis that links Senses, Syntactic Behavior and examples pertaining to different languages. "Axis" is a

[3] Morphology, Syntax and Semantic packages are described in [Francopoulo].

term taken from the Papillon[4] project [Sérasset 2001][5]. Axis can be organized at the lexicon manager convenience in order to link directly or indirectly objects of different languages.

6.1 Considerations for standardizing multilingual data

The simplest configuration of multilingual data is a bilingual lexicon where a single link is used to represent the translation of a given form/sense pair from one language into another. But a survey of actual practices clearly reveals other requirements that make the model more complex. Consequently, LMF has focused on the following ones:

(i) Cases where the relation 1-to-1 is impossible because of lexical differences among languages. An example is the case of English word “river” that relates to French words “rivière” and “fleuve”, where the latter is used for specifying that the referent is a river that flows into the sea. The bilingual lexicon should specify how these units relate.

(ii) The bilingual lexicon approach should be optimized to allow the easiest management of large databases for real multilingual scenarios. In order to reduce the explosion of links in a multi-bilingual scenario, translation equivalence can be managed through an intermediate "Axis". This object can be shared in order to contain the number of links in manageable proportions.

(iii) The model should cover both *transfer* and *pivot* approaches to translation, taking also into account hybrid approaches. In LMF, the pivot approach is implemented by a “Sense Axis”. The transfer approach is implemented by a “Transfer Axis”.

(iv) A situation that is not very easy to deal with is how to represent translations to languages that are similar or variants. The problem arises, for instance, when the task is to represent translations from English to both European Portuguese and Brazilian Portuguese. It is difficult to consider them as two separate languages. In fact, one is a variant of the other. The differences are minor: a certain number of words are different and some limited phenomena in syntax are different. Instead of managing two distinct copies, it is more effective to manage one lexicon with some objects that are marked with a dialectal attribute. Concerning the translation from English to Portuguese: a limited number of specific Axis instances record this variation and the vast majority of Axis instances is shared.

(v) The model should allow for representing the information that restricts or conditions the translations. The representation of tests that combine logical operations upon syntactic and semantic features must be covered.

6.2 Structure

The model is based on the notion of Axis that link Senses, Syntactic Behavior and examples pertaining to different languages. Axis can be organized at the lexicon manager convenience in order to link directly or indirectly objects of different languages. A direct link is implemented by a single axis. An indirect link is implemented by several axis and one or several relations.

The model is based on three main classes: Sense Axis, Transfer Axis, Example Axis.

6.3 Sense Axis

Sense Axis is used to link closely related senses in different languages, under the same assumptions of the interlingual pivot approach, and, optionally, it can also be used to refer to one or several external knowledge representation systems.

The use of the *Sense Axis* facilitates the representation of the translation of words that do not necessarily have the same valence or morphological form in one language than in another. For example, in a language, we can have a single word that will be translated by a compound word into another language: English “wheelchair” to Spanish “silla de ruedas”. *Sense Axis* may have the following attributes: a label, the name of an external descriptive system, a reference to a specific node inside an external description.

6.4 Sense Axis Relation

Sense Axis Relation permits to describe the linking between two different *Sense Axis* instances. The element may have attributes like label, view, etc.

[4] www.papillon-dictionary.org

[5] To be more precise, Papillon uses the term "axie" from "axis" and "lexie". In the beginning of the LMF project, we used the term "axie" but after some bad comments about using a non-English term in a standard, we decided to use the term "axis".

The label enables the coding of simple interlingual relations like the specialization of "fleuve" compared to "rivière" and "river". It is not, however, the goal of this strategy to code a complex system for knowledge representation, which ideally should be structured as a complete coherent system designed specifically for that purpose.

6.5 Transfer Axis

Transfer Axis is designed to represent multilingual transfer approach. Here, linkage refers to information contained in syntax. For example, this approach enables the representation of syntactic actants involving inversion, such as (1):

(1) `fra:"elle me manque" => eng:"I miss her"`

Due to the fact that a lexical entry can be a support verb, it is possible to represent translations that start from a plain verb to a support verb like (2) that means "Mary dreams":

(2) `fra:"Marie rêve" => jpn:"Marie wa yume wo miru"`

6.6 Transfer Axis Relation

Transfer Axis Relation links two *Transfer Axis* instances. The element may have attributes like: label, variation.

6.7 Source Test and Target Test

Source Test permits to express a condition on the translation on the source language side while *Target Test* does it on the target language side. Both elements may have attributes like: text and comment.

6.8 Example Axis

Example Axis supplies documentation for sample translations. The purpose is not to record large scale multilingual corpora. The goal is to link a Lexical Entry with a typical example of translation. The element may have attributes like: comment, source.

6.9 Class Model Diagram

The UML class model is an UML package. The diagram for multilingual notations is as follows:

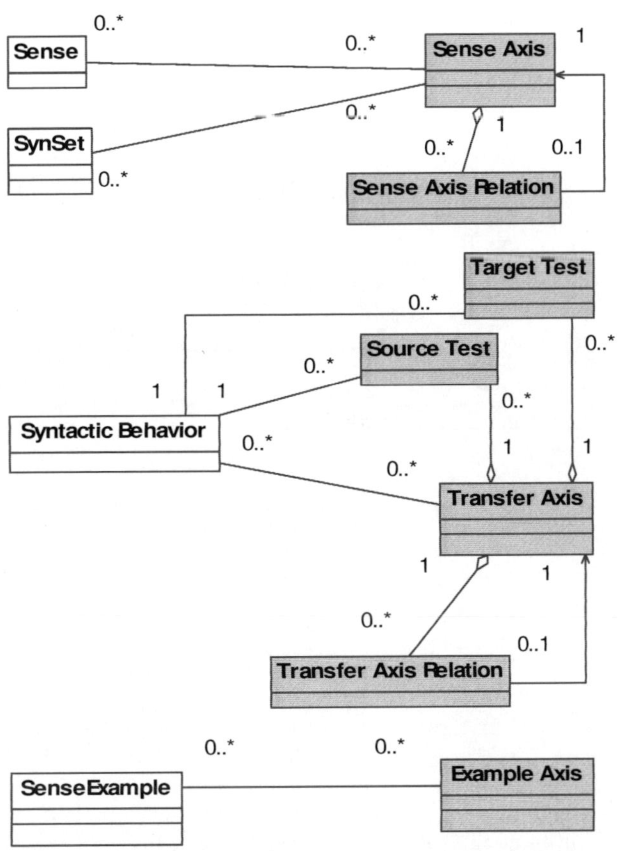

7 Three examples

7.1 First example

The first example is about the interlingual approach with two axis instances to represent a near match between "fleuve" in French and "river" in English. In the diagram, French is located on the left side and English on the right side. The axis on the top is not linked directly to any English sense because this notion does not exist in English.

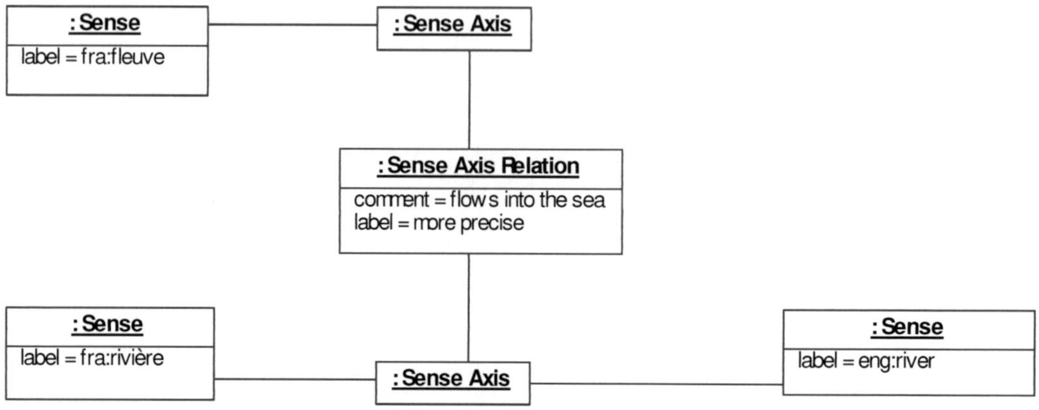

7.2 Second example

Let's see now an example about the transfer approach about slight variations between variants. The example is about English on one side and European Portuguese and Brazilian on the other side. Due to the fact that these two last variants have a very similar syntax, but with some local exceptions, the goal is to avoid a full and dummy duplication. For instance, the nominative forms of the third person clitics are largely preferred in Brazilian rather than the oblique form as in European Portuguese. The transfer axis relations hold a label to distinguish which axis to use depending on the target object.

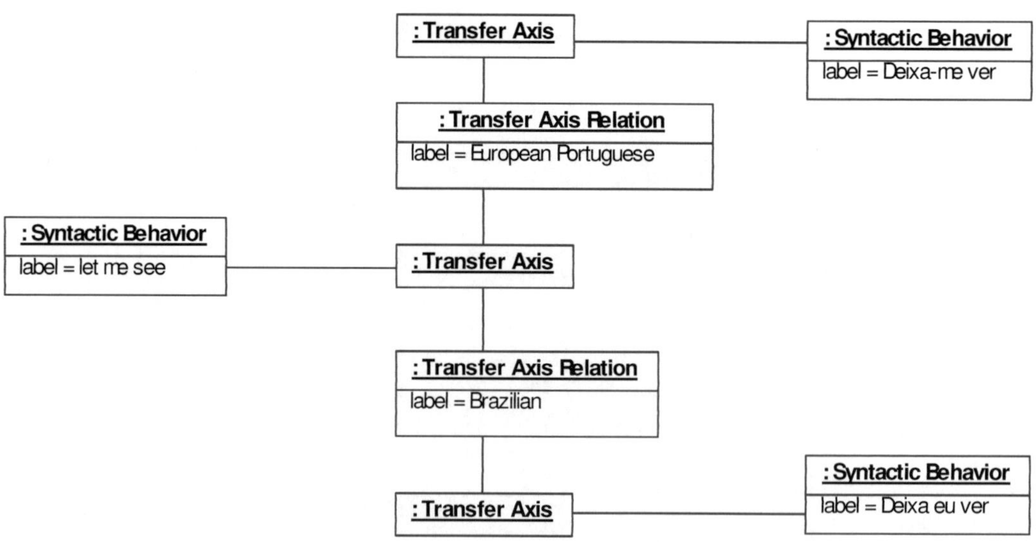

7.3 Third example

A third example shows how to use the Transfer Axis relation to relate different information in a multilingual transfer lexicon. It represents the translation of the English “develop” into Italian and Spanish. Recall that the more general sense links “eng:develop” and “esp:desarrollar”. Both, Spanish and Italian, have restrictions that should be tested in the source language: if the second argument of the construction refers to certain elements (picture, mentalCreation, building) it should be translated into specific verbs.

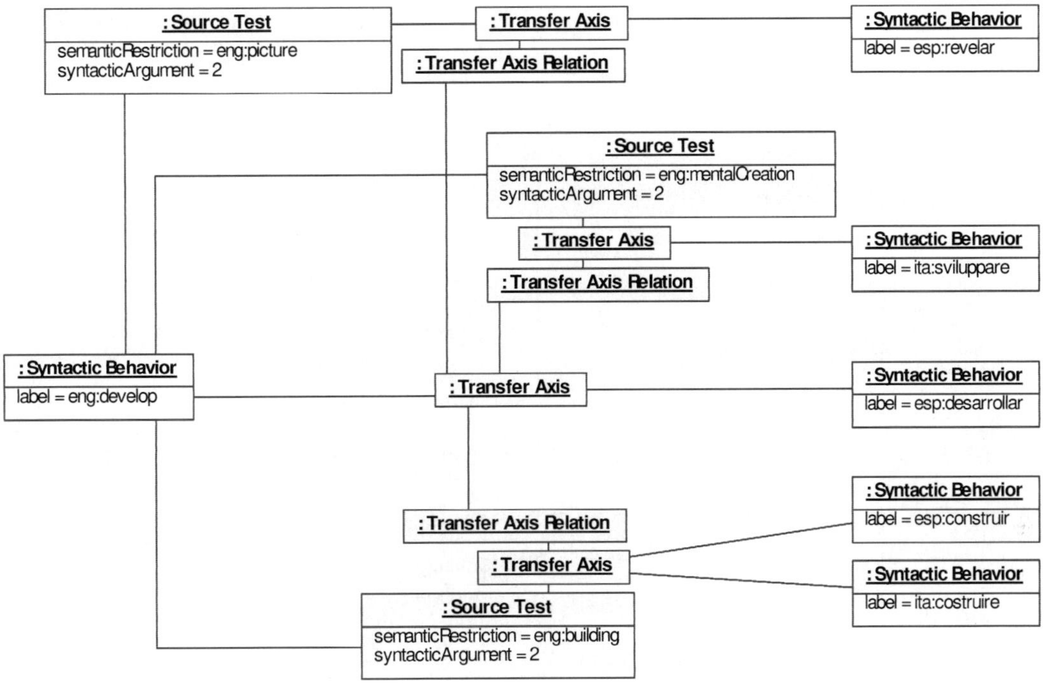

8 LMF in XML

During the last three years, the ISO group focused on the UML specification. In the last version of the LMF document [LMF 2006] a DTD has been provided as an informative annex. The following conventions are adopted:

- each UML attribute is transcoded as a DC (for Data Category) element
- each UML class is transcoded as an XML element
- UML aggregations are transcoded as content inclusion
- UML shared associations (i.e. associations that are not aggregations) are transcoded as IDREF(S)

The first example (i.e. "river") can be represented with the following XML tags:

```
<Database>
<!—                    French section →
<Lexicon>
<LexiconInformation>
    <DC att="name" val="French Extract"/>
    <DC att="language" val="fra"/>
</LexiconInformation>
<LexicalEntry >
    <DC att="partOfSpeech" val="noun"/>
    <LemmatisedForm>
        <DC att="writtenForm" val="fleuve"/>
    </LemmatisedForm>
    <Sense id="fra.fleuve1">
        <SemanticDefinition>
        <DC att="text"
        val="Grande rivière lorsqu'elle aboutit à la mer"/>
        <DC att="source" val="Le Petit Robert 2003"/>
        </SemanticDefinition>
    </Sense>
</LexicalEntry>
<LexicalEntry>
    <DC att="partOfSpeech" val="noun"/>
    <LemmatisedForm>
        <DC att="writtenForm" val="rivière"/>
    </LemmatisedForm>
    <Sense id="fra.riviere1">
        <SemanticDefinition>
        <DC att="text"
        val="Cours d'eau naturel de moyenne importance"/>
        <DC att="source" val="Le Petit Robert 2003"/>
        </SemanticDefinition>
    </Sense>
</LexicalEntry>
</Lexicon>
<!—                    Multilingual section →
<SenseAxis id="A1" senses="fra.fleuve1">
```

```
        <SenseAxisRelation targets="A2">
                <DC att="comment" val="flows into the sea"/>
                <DC att="label" val="more precise"/>
        </SenseAxisRelation>
</SenseAxis>
<SenseAxis id="A2" senses="fra.riviere1 eng.river1"/>
<!—                                English section →
<Lexicon>
<LexiconInformation>
        <DC att="name" val="English Extract"/>
        <DC att="language" val="eng"/>
</LexiconInformation>
<LexicalEntry>
        <DC att="partOfSpeech" val="noun"/>
        <LemmatisedForm>
                <DC att="writtenForm" val="river"/>
        </LemmatisedForm>
        <Sense id="eng.river1">
                <SemanticDefinition>
                <DC att="text"
                val="A natural and continuous flow of water in a long
line across a country into the sea"/>
                <DC att="source" val="Longman DCE 2005"/>
                </SemanticDefinition>
        </Sense>
</LexicalEntry>
</Lexicon>
</Database>
```

9 Comparison

A serious comparison with previously existing models is not possible in this current paper due to the lack of space. We advice the interested colleague to consult the technical report "Extended examples of lexicons using LMF" located at: "http://lirics.loria.fr" in the document area. The report explains how to use LMF in order to represent OLIF-2, Parole/Clips, LC-Star, WordNet, FrameNet and BDéf.

10 Conclusion

In this paper we presented the results of the ongoing research activity of the LMF ISO standard. The design of a common and standardized framework for multilingual lexical databases will contribute to the optimization of the use of lexical resources, specially their reusability for different applications and tasks. Interoperability is the condition of a effective deployment of usable lexical resources.

In order to reach a consensus, the work done has paid attention to the similarities and differences of existing lexicons and the models behind them.

Acknowledgements

The work presented here is partially funded by the EU eContent-22236 LIRICS project[6], partially by the French TECHNOLANGUE[7] + OUTILEX[8] programs.

References

Antoni-Lay M-H., Francopoulo G., Zaysser L. 1994 A generic model for reusable lexicons: the GENELEX project. Literary and linguistic computing 9(1) 47-54

Bertagna F., Lenci A., Monachini M., Calzolari N. 2004 Content interoperability of lexical resources, open issues and MILE perspectives LREC Lisbon

Francopoulo G., George M., Calzolari N., Monachini M., Bel N., Pet M., Soria C. 2006 Lexical Markup Framework (LMF) LREC Genoa.

LMF 2006 Lexical Markup Framework ISO-CD24613-revision-9, ISO Geneva

Rumbaugh J., Jacobson I.,Booch G. 2004 The unified modeling language reference manual, second edition, Addison Wesley

Sérasset G., Mangeot-Lerebours M. 2001 Papillon Lexical Database project: monolingual dictionaries & interlingual links NLPRS Tokyo

[6] http://lirics.loria.fr
[7] www.technolangue.net
[8] www.at-lci.com/outilex/outilex.html

The Role of Lexical Resources in CJK Natural Language Processing

Jack Halpern（春遍雀來）
The CJK Dictionary Institute (CJKI) (日中韓辭典研究所)
34-14, 2-chome, Tohoku, Niiza-shi, Saitama 352-0001, Japan
jack@cjk.org

Abstract

The role of lexical resources is often understated in NLP research. The complexity of Chinese, Japanese and Korean (CJK) poses special challenges to developers of NLP tools, especially in the area of word segmentation (WS), information retrieval (IR), named entity extraction (NER), and machine translation (MT). These difficulties are exacerbated by the lack of comprehensive lexical resources, especially for proper nouns, and the lack of a standardized orthography, especially in Japanese. This paper summarizes some of the major linguistic issues in the development NLP applications that are dependent on lexical resources, and discusses the central role such resources should play in enhancing the accuracy of NLP tools.

1 Introduction

Developers of CJK NLP tools face various challenges, some of the major ones being:

1. Identifying and processing the large number of orthographic variants in Japanese, and alternate character forms in CJK languages.
2. The lack of easily available comprehensive lexical resources, especially lexical databases, comparable to the major European languages.
3. The accurate conversion between Simplified and Traditional Chinese (Halpern and Kerman 1999).
4. The morphological complexity of Japanese and Korean.
5. Accurate word segmentation (Emerson 2000 and Yu et al. 2000) and disambiguating ambiguous segmentations strings (ASS) (Zhou and Yu 1994).
6. The difficulty of lexeme-based retrieval and CJK CLIR (Goto et al. 2001).
7. Chinese and Japanese proper nouns, which are very numerous, are difficult to detect without a lexicon.
8. Automatic recognition of terms and their variants (Jacquemin 2001).

The various attempts to tackle these tasks by statistical and algorithmic methods (Kwok 1997) have had only limited success. An important motivation for such methodology has been the poor availability and high cost of acquiring and maintaining large-scale lexical databases.

This paper discusses how a lexicon-driven approach exploiting large-scale lexical databases can offer reliable solutions to some of the principal issues, based on over a decade of experience in building such databases for NLP applications.

2 Named Entity Extraction

Named Entity Recognition (NER) is useful in NLP applications such as question answering, machine translation and information extraction. A major difficulty in NER, and a strong motivation for using tools based on probabilistic methods, is that the compilation and maintenance of large entity databases is time consuming and expensive. The number of personal names and their variants (e.g. over a hundred ways to spell *Mohammed*) is probably in the billions. The number of place names is also large, though they are relatively stable compared with the names of organizations and products, which change frequently.

A small number of organizations, including The CJK Dictionary Institute (CJKI), maintain databases of millions of proper nouns, but even such comprehensive databases cannot be kept fully up-to-date as countless new names are created daily. Various techniques have been used to automatically detect entities, one being the use of keywords or syntactic structures that co-occur with proper nouns, which we refer to as *named entity contextual clues* (NECC).

Proceedings of the Workshop on Multilingual Language Resources and Interoperability, pages 9–16,
Sydney, July 2006.

Table 1. Named Entity Contextual Clues

Headword	Reading	Example
センター	せんたー	国民生活**センター**
ホテル	ほてる	**ホテル**シオノ
駅	えき	朝霞**駅**
協会	きょうかい	日本ユニセフ**協会**

Table 1 shows NECCs for Japanese proper nouns, which when used in conjunction with entity lexicons like the one shown in Table 2 below achieve high precision in entity recognition. Of course for NER there is no need for such lexicons to be multilingual, though it is obviously essential for MT.

Table 2. Multilingual Database of Place Names

English	Japanese	Simplified Chinese	LO	Traditional Chinese	Korean
Azerbaijan	アゼルバイジャン	阿塞拜疆	L	亞塞拜然	아제르바이잔
Caracas	カラカス	加拉加斯	L	卡拉卡斯	카라카스
Cairo	カイロ	开罗	O	開羅	카이로
Chad	チャド	乍得	L	查德	차드
New Zealand	ニュージーランド	新西兰	L	紐西蘭	뉴질랜드
Seoul	ソウル	首尔	O	首爾	서울
Seoul	ソウル	汉城	O	漢城	서울
Yemen	イエメン	也门	L	葉門	예멘

Note how the lexemic pairs ("L" in the **LO** column) in Table 2 above are not merely simplified and traditional *orthographic* ("O") versions of each other, but independent lexemes equivalent to American *truck* and British *lorry.*

NER, especially of personal names and place names, is an area in which lexicon-driven methods have a clear advantage over probabilistic methods and in which the role of lexical resources should be a central one.

3 Linguistic Issues in Chinese

3.1 Processing Multiword Units

A major issue for Chinese segmentors is how to treat compound words and multiword lexical units (MWU), which are often decomposed into their components rather than treated as single units. For example, 录像带 *lùxiàngdài* 'video cassette' and 机器翻译 *jīqifānyì* 'machine translation' are not tagged as segments in Chinese Gigaword, the largest tagged Chinese corpus in existence, processed by the CKIP morphological analyzer (Ma 2003). Possible reasons for this include:

1. The lexicons used by Chinese segmentors are small-scale or incomplete. Our testing of various Chinese segmentors has shown that coverage of MWUs is often limited.
2. Chinese linguists disagree on the concept of wordhood in Chinese. Various theories such as the Lexical Integrity Hypothesis (Huang 1984) have been proposed. Packard's outstanding book (Packard 98) on the subject clears up much of the confusion.
3. The "correct" segmentation can depend on the application, and there are various segmentation standards. For example, a search engine user looking for 录像带 is not normally interested in 录像 'to videotape' and 带 'belt' per se, unless they are part of 录像带.

This last point is important enough to merit elaboration. A user searching for 中国人 *zhōngguórén* 'Chinese (person)' is *not* interested in 中国 'China', and vice-versa. A search for 中国 should *not* retrieve 中国人 as an instance of 中国. Exactly the same logic should apply to 机器翻译, so that a search for that keyword should only retrieve documents containing that string in its entirety. Yet performing a Google search on 机器翻译 in normal mode gave some 2.3 million hits, hundreds of thousands of which had zero occurrences of 机器翻译 but numerous occurrences of unrelated words like 机器人 'robot', which the user is not interested in.

This is equivalent to saying that *headwaiter* should not be considered an instance of *waiter*, which is indeed how Google behaves. More to the point, English space-delimited lexemes like *high school* are not instances of the adjective *high*. As shown in Halpern (2000b), "the degree of solidity often has nothing to do with the status of a string as a lexeme. *School bus* is just as legitimate a lexeme as is *headwaiter* or *word-processor*. The presence or absence of spaces or hyphens, that is, the orthography, does not determine the lexemic status of a string."

In a similar manner, it is perfectly legitimate to consider Chinese MWUs like those shown below as indivisible units for most applications, especially information retrieval and machine translation.

丝绸之路 *sīchóuzhīlù* silk road
机器翻译 *jīqìfānyì* machine translation
爱国主义 *àiguózhǔyì* patriotism
录像带 *lùxiàngdài* video cassette
新西兰 *Xīnxīlán* New Zealand
临阵磨枪 *línzhènmóqiāng*
start to prepare at the last moment

One could argue that 机器翻译 is compositional and therefore should be considered "two words." Whether we count it as one or two "words" is not really relevant – what matters is that it is *one lexeme* (smallest distinctive units associating meaning with form). On the other extreme, it is clear that idiomatic expressions like 临阵磨枪, literally "sharpen one's spear before going to battle," meaning 'start to prepare at the last moment,' are indivisible units.

Predicting compositionality is not trivial and often impossible. For many purposes, the only practical solution is to consider all lexemes as indivisible. Nonetheless, currently even the most advanced segmentors fail to identify such lexemes and missegment them into their constituents, no doubt because they are not registered in the lexicon. This is an area in which expanded lexical resources can significantly improve segmentation accuracy.

In conclusion, lexical items like 机器翻译 'machine translation' represent stand-alone, well-defined concepts and should be treated as single units. The fact that in English *machineless* is spelled solid and *machine translation* is not is an historical accident of orthography unrelated to the fundamental fact that both are full-fledged lexemes each of which represents an indivisible, independent concept. The same logic applies to 机器翻译, which is a full-fledged lexeme that should not be decomposed.

3.2 Multilevel Segmentation

Chinese MWUs can consist of nested components that can be segmented in different ways for different levels to satisfy the requirements of different segmentation standards. The example below shows how 北京日本人学校 *Běijīng Rìběnrén Xuéxiào* 'Beijing School for Japanese (nationals)' can be segmented on five different levels.

1. 北京日本人学校 multiword lexemic
2. 北京+日本人+学校 lexemic
3. 北京+日本+人+学校 sublexemic
4. 北京 + [日本 + 人] [学+校] morphemic
5. [北+京] [日+本+人] [学+校] submorphemic

For some applications, such as MT and NER, the multiword lexemic level is most appropriate (the level most commonly used in CJKI's dictionaries). For others, such as embedded speech technology where dictionary size matters, the lexemic level is best. A more advanced and expensive solution is to store presegmented MWUs in the lexicon, or even to store nesting delimiters as shown above, making it possible to select the desired segmentation level.

The problem of incorrect segmentation is especially obvious in the case of neologisms. Of course no lexical database can expect to keep up with the latest neologisms, and even the first edition of Chinese Gigaword does not yet have 博客 *bókè* 'blog'. Here are some examples of MWU neologisms, some of which are not (at least bilingually), compositional but fully qualify as lexemes.

电脑迷 *diànnǎomí* cyberphile
电子商务 *diànzǐshāngwù* e-commerce
追车族 *zhuīchēzú* auto fan

3.3 Chinese-to-Chinese Conversion (C2C)

Numerous Chinese characters underwent drastic simplifications in the postwar period. Chinese written in these simplified forms is called Simplified Chinese (SC). Taiwan, Hong Kong, and most overseas Chinese continue to use the old, complex forms, referred to as Traditional Chinese (TC). Contrary to popular perception, the process of accurately converting SC to/from TC is full of complexities and pitfalls. The linguistic issues are discussed in Halpern and Kerman (1999), while technical issues are described in Lunde (1999). The conversion can be implemented on three levels in increasing order of sophistication:

1. Code Conversion. The easiest, but most unreliable, way to perform C2C is to transcode by using a one-to-one mapping table. Because of the numerous one-to-many ambiguities, as shown below, the rate of conversion failure is unacceptably high.

Table 3. Code Conversion

SC	TC1	TC2	TC3	TC4	Remarks
门	們				one-to-one
汤	湯				one-to-one
发	發	髮			one-to-many
暗	暗	闇			one-to-many
干	幹	乾	干	榦	one-to-many

2. Orthographic Conversion. The next level of sophistication is to convert orthographic units, rather than codepoints. That is, meaningful linguistic units, equivalent to lexemes, with the important difference that the TC is the traditional version of the SC on a character form level. While code conversion is ambiguous, orthographic conversion gives much better results because the orthographic mapping tables enable conversion on the lexeme level, as shown below.

Table 4. Orthographic Conversion

English	SC	TC1	TC2	Incorrect
Telephone	电话	電話		
Dry	干燥	乾燥		干燥 幹燥 榦燥
	阴干	陰乾	陰干	

As can be seen, the ambiguities inherent in code conversion are resolved by using orthographic mapping tables, which avoids false conversions such as shown in the **Incorrect** column. Because of segmentation ambiguities, such conversion must be done with a segmentor that can break the text stream into meaningful units (Emerson 2000).

An extra complication, among various others, is that some lexemes have one-to-many orthographic mappings, *all* of which are correct. For example, SC 阴干 correctly maps to both TC 陰乾 'dry in the shade' and TC 陰干 'the five even numbers'. Well designed orthographic mapping tables must take such anomalies into account.

3. Lexemic Conversion. The most sophisticated form of C2C conversion is called *lexemic conversion,* which maps SC and TC lexemes that are semantically, not orthographically, equivalent. For example, SC 信息 *xìnxī* 'information' is converted into the semantically equivalent TC 資訊 *zīxùn*. This is similar to the difference between British *pavement* and American *sidewalk.* Tsou (2000) has demonstrated that there are numerous lexemic differences between SC and TC, especially in technical terms and proper nouns, e.g. there are more than 10 variants for *Osama bin Laden.*

Table 5. Lexemic Conversion

English	SC	Taiwan TC	HK TC	Incorrect TC
Software	软件	軟體	軟件	軟件
Taxi	出租汽车	計程車	的士	出租汽車
Osama Bin Laden	奥萨马本拉登	奧薩瑪賓拉登	奧薩瑪賓拉丹	奧薩馬本拉登
Oahu	瓦胡岛	歐胡島		瓦胡島

3.4 Traditional Chinese Variants

Traditional Chinese has numerous variant character forms, leading to much confusion. Disambiguating these variants can be done by using mapping tables such as the one shown below. If such a table is carefully constructed by limiting it to cases of 100% semantic interchangeability for polysemes, it is easy to normalize a TC text by trivially replacing variants by their standardized forms. For this to work, all relevant components, such as MT dictionaries, search engine indexes and the related documents should be normalized. An extra complication is that Taiwanese and Hong Kong variants are sometimes different (Tsou 2000).

Table 6. TC Variants

Var. 1	Var. 2	English	Comment
裏	裡	Inside	100% interchangeable
著	着	Particle	variant 2 not in Big5
沉	沈	sink; surname	partially interchangeable

4 Orthographic Variation in Japanese

4.1 Highly Irregular Orthography

The Japanese orthography is highly irregular, significantly more so than any other major language, including Chinese. A major factor is the complex interaction of the four scripts used to write Japanese, e.g. kanji, hiragana, katakana, and the Latin alphabet, resulting in countless words that can be written in a variety of often unpredictable ways, and the lack of a standardized orthography. For example, *toriatsukai* 'handling' can be written in six ways: 取り扱い, 取扱い, 取扱, とり扱い, 取りあつかい, とりあつかい.

An example of how difficult Japanese IR can be is the proverbial 'A hen that lays golden eggs.' The "standard" orthography would be 金の卵を産む鶏 *Kin no tamago o umu niwatori.* In reality, *tamago* 'egg' has four variants (卵, 玉子, たまご, タマゴ), *niwatori* 'chicken' three (鶏, にわとり, ニワトリ) and *umu* 'to lay' two (産む, 生む), which expands to 24 permutations like 金の卵を生むニワトリ, 金の玉子を産む鶏 etc. As can be easily verified by searching the web, these variants occur frequently.

Linguistic tools that perform segmentation, MT, entity extraction and the like must identify and/or normalize such variants to perform dictionary lookup. Below is a brief discussion of what kind of variation occurs and how such normalization can be achieved.

4.2 Okurigana Variants

One of the most common types of orthographic variation in Japanese occurs in kana endings, called *okurigana*, that are attached to a kanji stem. For example, *okonau* 'perform' can be written 行う or 行なう, whereas *toriatsukai* can be written in the six ways shown above. Okurigana variants are numerous and unpredictable. Identifying them must play a major role in Japanese orthographic normalization. Although it is possible to create a dictionary of okurigana variants algorithmically, the resulting lexicon would be huge and may create numerous false positives not semantically interchangeable. The most effective solution is to use a lexicon of okurigana variants, such as the one shown below:

Table 7. Okurigana Variants

HEADWORD	READING	NORMALIZED
書き著す	かきあらわす	書き著す
書き著わす	かきあらわす	書き著す
書著す	かきあらわす	書き著す
書著わす	かきあらわす	書き著す

Since Japanese is highly agglutinative and verbs can have numerous inflected forms, a lexicon such as the above must be used in conjunction with a morphological analyzer that can do accurate stemming, i.e. be capable of recognizing that 書き著しませんでした is the polite form of the canonical form 書き著す.

4.3 Cross-Script Orthographic Variation

Variation across the four scripts in Japanese is common and unpredictable, so that the same word can be written in any of several scripts, or even as a hybrid of multiple scripts, as shown below:

Table 8. Cross-Script Variation

Kanji	Hiragana	katakana	Latin	Hybrid	Gloss
人参	にんじん	ニンジン			carrot
		オープン	OPEN		open
硫黄		イオウ			sulfur
		ワイシャツ		Y シャツ	shirt
皮膚		ヒフ		皮フ	skin

Cross-script variation can have major consequences for recall, as can be seen from the table below.

Table 9: Hit Distribution for 人参 'carrot' *ninjin*

ID	Keyword	Normalized	Google Hits
A	人参	人参	67,500
B	にんじん	人参	66,200
C	ニンジン	人参	58,000

Using the ID above to represent the number of Google hits, this gives a total of $A+B+C+\alpha_{123} = 191{,}700$. α is a coincidental occurrence factor, such as in '100 人参加, in which '人参' is unrelated to the 'carrot' sense. The formulae for calculating the above are as follows.

Unnormalized recall:

$$\frac{C}{A+B+C+\alpha_{123}} = \frac{58,000}{191,700} \ (\approx 30\%)$$

Normalized recall:

$$\frac{A+B+C}{A+B+C+\alpha_{123}} = \frac{191,700}{191,700} \ (\approx 100\%)$$

Unnormalized precision:

$$\frac{C}{C+\alpha_{3}} = \frac{58,000}{58,000} \ (\approx 100\%)$$

Normalized precision:

$$\frac{C}{A+B+C+\alpha_{123}} = \frac{191,700}{191,700} \ (\approx 100\%)$$

人参 'carrot' illustrates how serious a problem cross-orthographic variants can be. If orthographic normalization is not implemented to ensure that all variants are indexed on a standardized form like 人参, recall is only 30%; if it is, there is a dramatic improvement and recall goes up to nearly 100%, without any loss in precision, which hovers at 100%.

4.4 Kana Variants

A sharp increase in the use of katakana in recent years is a major annoyance to NLP applications because katakana orthography is often irregular; it is quite common for the same word to be written in multiple, unpredictable ways. Although hiragana orthography is generally regular, a small number of irregularities persist. Some of the major types of kana variation are shown in the table below.

Table 10. Kana Variants

Type	English	Standard	Variants
Macron	computer	コンピュータ	コンピューター
Long vowels	maid	メード	メイド
Multiple kana	team	チーム	ティーム
Traditional	big	おおきい	おうきい
づ vs. ず	continue	つづく	つずく

The above is only a brief introduction to the most important types of kana variation. Though attempts at algorithmic solutions have been made by some NLP research laboratories (Brill 2001), the most practical solution is to use a katakana normalization table, such as the one shown below, as is being done by Yahoo! Japan and other major portals.

Table 11. Kana Variants

HEADWORD	NORMALIZED	English
アーキテクチャ	アーキテクチャー	Architecture
アーキテクチャー	アーキテクチャー	Architecture
アーキテクチュア	アーキテクチャー	Architecture

4.5 Miscellaneous Variants

There are various other types of orthographic variants in Japanese, described in Halpern (2000a). To mention some, kanji even in contemporary Japanese sometimes have variants, such as 才 for 歳 and 巾 for 幅, and traditional forms such as 發 for 発. In addition, many *kun* homophones and their variable orthography are often close or even identical in meaning, i.e., *noboru* means 'go up' when written 上る but 'climb' when written 登る, so that great care must be taken in the normalization process so as to assure semantic interchangeability for all senses of polysemes; that is, to ensure that such forms are *excluded* from the normalization table.

4.6 Lexicon-driven Normalization

Leaving statistical methods aside, lexicon-driven normalization of Japanese orthographic variants can be achieved by using an orthographic mapping table such as the one shown below, using various techniques such as:

1. Convert variants to a standardized form for indexing.
2. Normalize queries for dictionary lookup.
3. Normalize all source documents.
4. Identify forms as members of a variant group.

Table 12. Orthographic Normalization Table

HEADWORD	READING	NORMALIZED
空き缶	あきかん	空き缶
空缶	あきかん	空き缶
明き罐	あきかん	空き缶
あき缶	あきかん	空き缶
あき罐	あきかん	空き缶
空きかん	あきかん	空き缶
空きカン	あきかん	空き缶
空き罐	あきかん	空き缶
空罐	あきかん	空き缶
空き鑵	あきかん	空き缶
空鑵	あきかん	空き缶

Other possibilities for normalization include advanced applications such as domain-specific synonym expansion, requiring Japanese thesauri based on domain ontologies, as is done by a select number of companies like Wand and Convera who build sophisticated Japanese IR systems.

5 Orthographic Variation in Korean

Modern Korean has is a significant amount of orthographic variation, though far less than in Japanese. Combined with the morphological complexity of the language, this poses various challenges to developers of NLP tools. The issues are similar to Japanese in principle but differ in detail.

Briefly, Korean has variant hangul spellings in the writing of loanwords, such as 케이크 *keikeu* and 케잌 *keik* for 'cake', and in the writing of non-Korean personal names, such as 클린턴 *keulrinteon* and 클린톤 *keulrinton* for 'Clinton'. In addition, similar to Japanese but on a smaller scale, Korean is written in a mixture of hangul, Chinese characters and the Latin alphabet. For example, 'shirt' can be written 와이셔츠 *wai-syeacheu* or Y 셔츠 *wai-syeacheu*, whereas 'one o'clock' *hanzi* can written as 한시, 1 시 or 一時. Another issue is the differences between South and North Korea spellings, such as N.K. 오사까 *osakka* vs. S.K. 오사카 *osaka* for 'Osaka', and the old (pre-1988) orthography versus the new, i.e. modern 일군 'worker' (*ilgun*) used to be written 일꾼 (*ilkkun*).

Lexical databases, such as normalization tables similar to the ones shown above for Japanese, are the only practical solution to identifying such variants, as they are in principle unpredictable.

6 The Role of Lexical Databases

Because of the irregular orthography of CJK languages, procedures such as orthographic normalization cannot be based on statistical and probabilistic methods (e.g. bigramming) alone, not to speak of pure algorithmic methods. Many attempts have been made along these lines, as for example Brill (2001) and Goto et al. (2001), with some claiming performance equivalent to lexicon-driven methods, while Kwok (1997) reports good results with only a small lexicon and simple segmentor.

Emerson (2000) and others have reported that a robust morphological analyzer capable of processing lexemes, rather than bigrams or n-grams, must be supported by a large-scale computational lexicon. This experience is shared by many of the world's major portals and MT developers, who make extensive use of lexical databases.

Unlike in the past, disk storage is no longer a major issue. Many researchers and developers, such as Prof. Franz Guenthner of the University of Munich, have come to realize that "language is in the data," and "the data is in the dictionary," even to the point of compiling full-form dictionaries with millions of entries rather than rely on statistical methods, such as Meaningful Machines who use a full form dictionary containing millions of entries in developing a human quality Spanish-to-English MT system.

CJKI, which specializes in CJK and Arabic computational lexicography, is engaged in an ongoing research and development effort to compile CJK and Arabic lexical databases (currently about seven million entries), with special emphasis on proper nouns, orthographic normalization, and C2C. These resources are being subjected to heavy industrial use under real-world conditions, and the feedback thereof is being used to further expand these databases and to enhance the effectiveness of the NLP tools based on them.

7 Conclusions

Performing such tasks as orthographic normalization and named entity extraction accurately is beyond the ability of statistical methods alone, not to speak of C2C conversion and morphological analysis. However, the small-scale lexical resources currently used by many NLP tools are inadequate to these tasks. Because of the irregular orthography of the CJK writing systems, lexical databases fine-tuned to the needs of NLP applications are required. The building of large-scale lexicons based on corpora consisting of even billions of words has come of age. Since lexicon-driven techniques have proven their effectiveness, there is no need to overly rely on probabilistic methods. Comprehensive, up-to-date lexical resources are the key to achieving major enhancements in NLP technology.

References

Brill, E. and Kacmarick, G. and Brocket, C. (2001) *Automatically Harvesting Katakana-English Term Pairs from Search Engine Query Logs*. Microsoft Research, Proc. of the Sixth Natural Language Processing Pacific Rim Symposium, Tokyo, Japan.

Packard, L. Jerome (1998) "New Approaches to Chinese Word Formation", Mouton Degruyter, Berlin and New York.

Emerson, T. (2000) *Segmenting Chinese in Unicode. Proc. of the 16th International Unicode Conference*, Amsterdam

Goto, I., Uratani, N. and Ehara T. (2001) *Cross-Language Information Retrieval of Proper Nouns using Context Information*. NHK Science and Technical Research Laboratories. Proc. of the Sixth Natural Language Processing Pacific Rim Symposium, Tokyo, Japan

Huang, James C. (1984) *Phrase Structure, Lexical Integrity, and Chinese Compounds,* Journal of the Chinese Teachers Language Association, 19.2: 53-78

Jacquemin, C. (2001) *Spotting and Discovering Terms through Natural Language Processing*. The MIT Press, Cambridge, MA

Halpern, J. and Kerman J. (1999) *The Pitfalls and Complexities of Chinese to Chinese Conversion*. Proc. of the Fourteenth International Unicode Conference in Cambridge, MA.

Halpern, J. (2000a) *The Challenges of Intelligent Japanese Searching*. Working paper (www.cjk.org/cjk/joa/joapaper.htm), The CJK Dictionary Institute, Saitama, Japan.

Halpern, J. (2000b) *Is English Segmentation Trivial?*. Working paper, (www.cjk.org/cjk/reference/engmorph.htm) The CJK Dictionary Institute, Saitama, Japan.

Kwok, K.L. (1997) *Lexicon Effects on Chinese Information Retrieval*. Proc. of 2nd Conf. on Empirical Methods in NLP. ACL. pp.141-8.

Lunde, Ken (1999) *CJKV Information Processing*. O'Reilly & Associates, Sebastopol, CA.

Yu, Shiwen, Zhu, Xue-feng and Wang, Hui (2000) *New Progress of the Grammatical Knowledge-base of Contemporary Chinese*. Journal of Chinese Information Processing, Institute of Computational Linguistics, Peking University, Vol.15 No.1.

Ma, Wei-yun and Chen, Keh-Jiann (2003) *Introduction to CKIP Chinese Word Segmentation System for the First International Chinese Word Segmentation Bakeoff,* Proceedings of the Second SIGHAN Workshop on Chinese Language Processingpp. 168-171 Sapporo, Japan

Yu, Shiwen, Zhu, Xue-feng and Wang, Hui (2000) *New Progress of the Grammatical Knowledge-base of Contemporary Chinese*. Journal of Chinese Information Processing, Institute of Computational Linguistics, Peking University, Vol.15 No.1.

Tsou, B.K., Tsoi, W.F., Lai, T.B.Y. Hu, J., and Chan S.W.K. (2000) *LIVAC, a Chinese synchronous corpus, and some applications*. In "2000 International Conference on Chinese Language ComputingICCLC2000", Chicago.

Zhou, Qiang. and Yu, Shiwen (1994) *Blending Segmentation with Tagging in Chinese Language Corpus Processing,* 15th International Conference on Computational Linguistics (COLING 1994)

Towards Agent-based Cross-lingual Interoperability of Distributed Lexical Resources

Claudia Soria* **Maurizio Tesconi°** **Andrea Marchetti°**
Francesca Bertagna* **Monica Monachini***
Chu-Ren Huang§ **Nicoletta Calzolari***

*CNR-ILC and °CNR-IIT
Via Moruzzi 1, 56024 Pisa
Italy
{firstname.lastname@ilc.cnr.it}
{firstname.lastname@iit.cnr.it}

§Academia Sinica
Nankang, Taipei
Taiwan
churen@gate.sinica.edu.tw

Abstract

In this paper we present an application fostering the integration and interoperability of computational lexicons, focusing on the particular case of mutual linking and cross-lingual enrichment of two wordnets, the ItalWordNet and Sinica BOW lexicons. This is intended as a case-study investigating the needs and requirements of semi-automatic integration and interoperability of lexical resources.

1 Introduction

In this paper we present an application fostering the integration and interoperability of computational lexicons, focusing on the particular case of mutual linking and cross-lingual enrichment of two wordnets. The development of this application is intended as a case-study and a test-bed for trying out needs and requirements posed by the challenge of semi-automatic integration and enrichment of practical, large-scale multilingual lexicons for use in computer applications. While a number of lexicons already exist, few of them are practically useful, either since they are not sufficiently broad or because they don't cover the necessary level of detailed information. Moreover, multilingual language resources are not as widely available and are very costly to construct: the work process for manual development of new lexical resources or for tailoring existing ones is too expensive in terms of effort and time to be practically attractive.

The need of ever growing lexical resources for effective multilingual content processing has urged the language resource community to call for a radical change in the perspective of language resource creation and maintenance and the design of a "new generation" of LRs: from static, closed and locally developed resources to shared and distributed language *services*, based on open content interoperability standards. This has often been called a "change in paradigm" (in the sense of Kuhn, see Calzolari and Soria, 2005; Calzolari 2006). Leaving aside the tantalizing task of building on-site resources, the new paradigm depicts a scenario where lexical resources are cooperatively built as the result of controlled co-operation of different agents, adopting the paradigm of accumulation of knowledge so successful in more mature disciplines, such as biology and physics (Calzolari, 2006).

According to this view (or, better, this *vision*), different lexical resources reside over distributed places and can not only be accessed but *choreographed* by agents presiding the actions that can be executed over them. This implies the ability to build on each other achievements, to merge results, and to have them accessible to various systems and applications.

At the same time, there is another argument in favor of distributed lexical resources: language resources, lexicons included, are inherently distributed because of the diversity of languages distributed over the world. It is not only natural that language resources to be developed and maintained in their native environment. Since language evolves and changes over time, it is not possible to describe the current state of the lan-

Proceedings of the Workshop on Multilingual Language Resources and Interoperability, pages 17–24,
Sydney, July 2006.

guage away from where the language is spoken. Lastly, the vast range of diversity of languages also makes it impossible to have one single universal centralized resource, or even a centralized repository of resources.

Although the paradigm of distributed and interoperable lexical resources has largely been discussed and invoked, very little has been made in comparison for the development of new methods and techniques for its practical realization. Some initial steps are made to design frameworks enabling inter-lexica access, search, integration and operability. An example is the Lexus tool (Kemps-Snijders et al., 2006), based on the Lexical Markup Framework (Romary et al., 2006), that goes in the direction of managing the exchange of data among large-scale lexical resources. A similar tool, but more tailored to the collaborative creation of lexicons for endangered language, is SHAWEL (Gulrajani and Harrison, 2002). However, the general impression is that little has been made towards the development of new methods and techniques for attaining a concrete interoperability among lexical resources. Admittedly, this is a long-term scenario requiring the contribution of many different actors and initiatives (among which we only mention standardisation, distribution and international cooperation).

Nevertheless, the intent of our project is to contribute to fill in this gap, by exploring in a controlled way the requirement and implications posed by new generation multilingual lexical resources. The paper is organized as follows: section 2 describes the general architectural design of our project; section 3 describes the module taking care of cross-lingual integration of lexical resources, by also presenting a case-study involving an Italian and Chinese lexicons. Finally, section 4 presents our considerations and lessons learned on the basis of this exploratory testing.

2 An Architecture for Integrating Lexical Resources

LeXFlow (Soria et al., 2006) was developed having in mind the long-term goal of lexical resource interoperability. In a sense, LeXFlow is intended as a proof of concept attempting to make the *vision* of an infrastructure for access and sharing of linguistic resources more tangible.

LeXFlow is an adaptation to computational lexicons of XFlow, a cooperative web application for the management of document workflows (DW, Marchetti et al., 2005). A DW can be seen as a process of cooperative authoring where a document can be the goal of the process or just a side effect of the cooperation. Through a DW, a document life-cycle is tracked and supervised, continually providing control over the actions leading to document compilation. In this environment a document travels among agents who essentially carry out the pipeline receive-process-send activity.

There are two types of agents: *external agents* are human or software actors performing activities dependent from the particular Document Workflow Type; *internal agents* are software actors providing general-purpose activities useful for many DWTs and, for this reason, implemented directly into the system. Internal agents perform general functionalities such as creating/converting a document belonging to a particular DW, populating it with some initial data, duplicating a document to be sent to multiple agents, splitting a document and sending portions of information to different agents, merging duplicated documents coming from multiple agents, aggregating fragments, and finally terminating operations over the document. External agents basically *execute* some processing using the document content and possibly other data; for instance, accessing an external database or launching an application.

LeXFlow was born by tailoring XFlow to management of lexical entries; in doing so, we have assumed that each lexical entry can be modelled as a document instance, whose behaviour can be formally specified by means of a *lexical workflow type* (LWT). A LWT describes the life-cycle of a lexical entry, the agents allowed to act over it, the actions to be performed by the agents, and the order in which the actions are to be executed. Embracing the view of cooperative workflows, agents can have different rights or views over the same entry: this nicely suits the needs of lexicographic work, where we can define different roles (such as encoder, annotator, validator) that can be played by either human or software agents. Other software modules can be inserted in the flow, such as an automatic acquirer of information from corpora or from the web. Moreover, deriving from a tool designed for the cooperation of agents, LeXFlow allows to manage workflows where the different agents can reside over distributed places.

LeXFlow thus inherits from XFlow the general design and architecture, and can be considered as a specialized version of it through design of specific Lexical Workflow Types and plug-in of dedicated external software agents. In the next section we briefly illustrate a particular Lexical Workflow Type and the external software agents developed for the purpose of integrating different lexicons belonging to the same language. Since it allows the independent and coordinated sharing of actions over portions of lexicons, LeXFlow naturally lends itself as a tool for the management of distributed lexical resources.

Due to its versatility, LeXFlow is both a general framework where ideas on automatic lexical resource integration can be tested and an infrastructure for proving new methods for cooperation among lexicon experts.

2.1 Using LeXFlow for Lexicon Enrichment

In previous work (Soria et al., 2006), the LeXFlow framework has been tested for integration of lexicons with differently conceived lexical architectures and diverging formats. It was shown how interoperability is possible between two Italian lexicons from the SIMPLE and WordNet families, respectively, namely the SIMPLE/CLIPS (Ruimy et al., 2003) and ItalWordNet (Roventini et al., 2003) lexicons.

In particular, a Lexical Workflow Type was designed where the two different monolingual semantic lexicons interact by reciprocally enriching themselves and moreover integrate information coming from corpora. This LWT, called "lexicon augmentation", explicitly addresses dynamic augmentation of semantic lexicons. In this scenario, an entry of a lexicon *A* becomes enriched via basically two steps. First, by virtue of being mapped onto a corresponding entry belonging to a lexicon *B*, the entry_A inherits the semantic relations available in the mapped entry_B. Second, by resorting to an automatic application that acquires information about semantic relations from corpora, the acquired relations are integrated into the entry and proposed to the human encoder.

An overall picture of the flow is shown in Figure 1, illustrating the different agents participating in the flow. Rectangles represent human actors over the entries, while the other figures symbolize software agents: ovals are internal agents and octagons external ones. The two external agents involved in this flow are the "relation calculator" and the "corpora extractor". The first is responsible for the mapping between the sets of semantic relations used by the different lexicons. The "corpora extractor" module invokes an application that acquires information

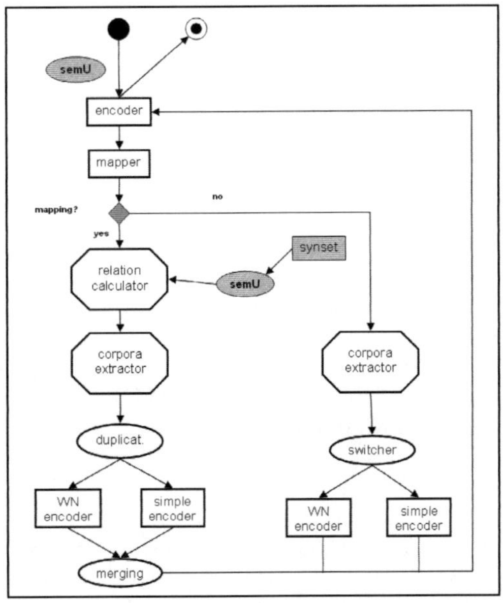

Figure 1. Lexicons Augmentation Workflow Type.

about *part-of* relations by identifying syntactic constructions in a vast Italian corpus. It then takes care of creating the appropriate candidate semantic relations for each lemma that is proposed by the application.

A prototype of LeXFlow has been implemented with an extensive use of XML technologies (XML Schema, XSLT, XPath, XForms, SVG) and open-source tools (Cocoon, Tomcat, mySQL). It is a web-based application where human agents interact with the system through an XForms browser that displays the document to process as a web form whereas software agents interact with the system via web services.

3 Multilingual WN Service

In the Section above we have illustrated the general architecture of LeXFlow and showed how a Lexical Workflow Type can be implemented in order to enrich already existing lexicons belonging to the same language but realizing different models of lexicon encoding. In this section we move to a cross-lingual perspective of lexicon integration. We present a module that similarly addresses the issue of lexicon augmentation or enrichment focusing on mutual enrichment of two wordnets in *different languages and residing at different sites*.

This module, named "multilingual WN Service" is responsible for the *automatic cross-lingual fertilization* of lexicons having a Word-

Net-like structure. Put it very simply, the idea behind this module is that a monolingual wordnet can be enriched by accessing the semantic information encoded in corresponding entries of other monolingual wordnets.

Since each entry in the monolingual lexicons is linked to the Interlingual Index (ILI, cf. Section 3.1), a synset of a WN(A) is indirectly linked to another synset in another WN(B). On the basis of this correspondence, a synset(A) can be enriched by importing the relations that the corresponding synset(B) holds with other synsets(B), and vice-versa. Moreover, the enrichment of WN(A) will not only import the relations found in WN(B), but it will also propose target synsets in the language(A) on the basis of those found in language(B).

The various WN lexicons reside over distributed servers and can be queried through web service interfaces. The overall architecture for multilingual wordnet service is depicted in Figure 2.

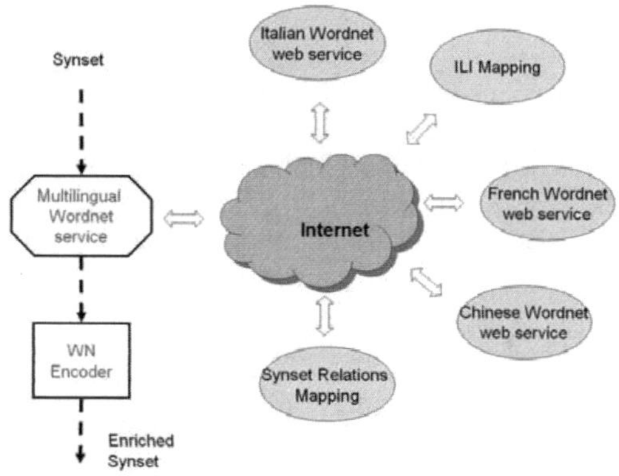

Figure 2. Multilingual Wordnet Service Architecture.

Put in the framework of the general LeXFlow architecture, the Multilingual wordnet Service can be seen as an additional external software agent that can be added to the augmentation workflow or included in other types of lexical flows. For instance, it can be used not only to enrich a monolingual lexicon but to bootstrap a bilingual lexicon.

3.1 Linking Lexicons through the ILI

The entire mechanism of the Multilingual WN Service is based on the exploitation of Interlingual Index (Peters et al., 1998), an unstructured version of WordNet used in EuroWordNet (Vossen et al., 1998) to link wordnets of different languages; each synset in the language-specific wordnet is linked to at least one record of the ILI by means of a set of equivalence relations (among which the most important is the EQ_SYNONYM, that expresses a total, perfect equivalence between two synsets).

Figure 6 describes the schema of a WN lexical entry. Under the root "synset" we find both internal relations ("synset relations") and ILI Relations, which link to ILI synsets.

Figure 3 shows the role played by the ILI as set of pivot nodes allowing the linkage between concepts belonging to different wordnets.

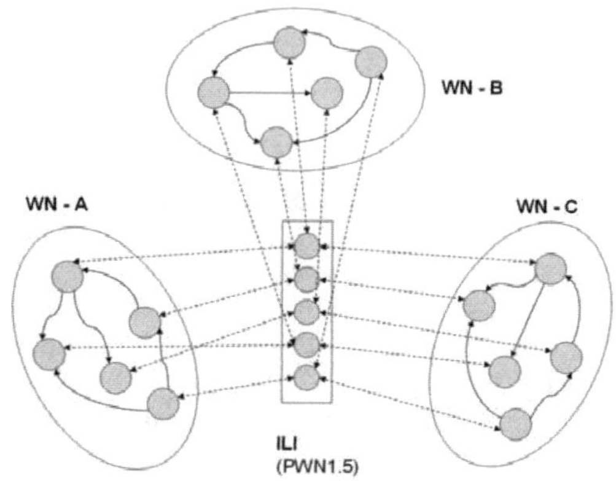

Figure 3. Interlingual Linking of Language-specific Synsets.

In the Multilingual WN Service, only equivalence relations of type EQ_SYNONYM and EQ_NEAR_SYNONYM have been taken into account, being them the ones used to represent a translation of concepts and also because they are the most exploited (for example, in IWN, they cover about the 60% of the encoded equivalence relations). The EQ_SYNONYM relation is used to realize the one-to-one mapping between the language-specific synset and the ILI, while multiple EQ_NEAR_SYNONYM relations (because of their nature) might be encoded to link a single language-specific synset to more than one ILI record. In Figure 4 we represented the possible relevant combinations of equivalence relations that can realize the mapping between synsets belonging to two languages. In all the four cases, a synset "a" is linked via the ILI record to a synset "b" but a specific procedure has been foreseen in order to calculate different "plausibility scores" to each situation. The procedure relies on different rates assigned to the two equivalence relations (rate "1" to EQ_NEAR_SYNONYM relation and rate "0" to the EQ_SYNONYM). In this way we can distinguish the four cases by assigning respectively a weight of "0", "1", "1" and "2".

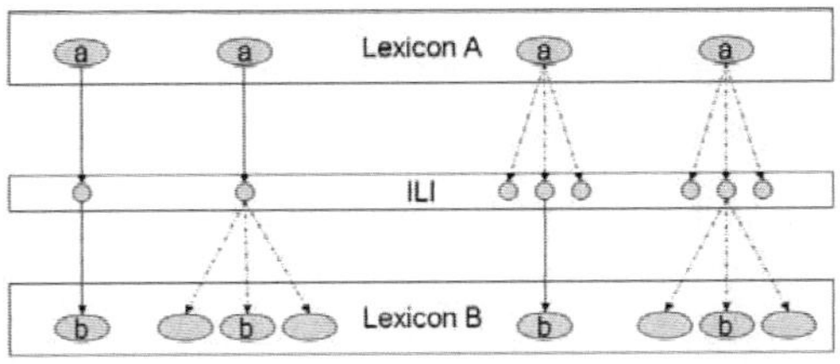

Figure 4. Possible Combinations of Relations between two Lexicons A and B and the ILI.

The ILI is a quite powerful yet simple method to link concepts across the many lexicons belonging to the *WordNet-family*. Unfortunately, no version of the ILI can be considered a standard and often the various lexicons exploit different version of WordNet as ILI[1]. This is a problem that is handled at web-service level, by incorporating the conversion tables provided by (Daudé et al., 2001). In this way, the use of different versions of WN does not have to be taken into consideration by the user who accesses the system but it is something that is resolved by the system itself[2]. This is why the version of the ILI is a parameter of the query to web service (see Section below).

3.2 Description of the Procedure

On the basis of ILI linking, a synset can be enriched by importing the relations contained in the corresponding synsets belonging to another wordnet.

In the procedure adopted, the enrichment is performed on a synset-by-synset basis. In other words, a certain synset is selected from a wordnet resource, say WN(A). The cross-lingual module identifies the corresponding ILI synset, on the basis of the information encoded in the synset. It then sends a query to the WN(B) web service providing the ID of ILI synset together with the ILI version of the starting WN. The WN(B) web service returns the synset(s) corresponding to the WN(A) synset, together with reliability scores. If WN(B) is based on a different ILI version, it can carry out the mapping between ILI versions (for instance by querying the ILI mapping web service). The cross-lingual module then analyzes the synset relations encoded in the WN(B) synset and for each of them creates a new synset relation for the WN(A) synset.

If the queried wordnets do not use the same set of synset relations, the module must take care of the mapping between different relation sets. In our case-study no mapping was needed, since the two sets were completely equivalent.

Each new relation is obtained by substituting the target WN(B) synset with the corresponding synset WN(A), which again is found by querying back the WN(A) web service (all these steps through the ILI). The procedure is formally defined by the following formula:

```
Let a_j ∈ A
Let Ba_j={b_i | b_i∈B and (b_i ILI a_j)}
∀ b_i∈Ba_j
   Let R_i={b_i r_k b_p | b_i,b_p∈B and (r_k ∈ R_A∩R_B)}
   ∀ b_i r_k b_p ∈ R_i
      Let Ab_p={a_i | a_i ∈ A and (a_i ILI b_p)}
      ∀ a_t ∈ Ab_p
         a_j r_k a_t is a candidate relation

Legenda:
A,B        lexicons
a_j,b_i    synsets
a_j r_p a_i  synset relation r_p between a_j and a_i
b_i ILI a_j  b_i is connected by ILI with a_j
R_A,R_B    relation space of lexicons B
R_A∩R_B    the common relation space of B and A
```

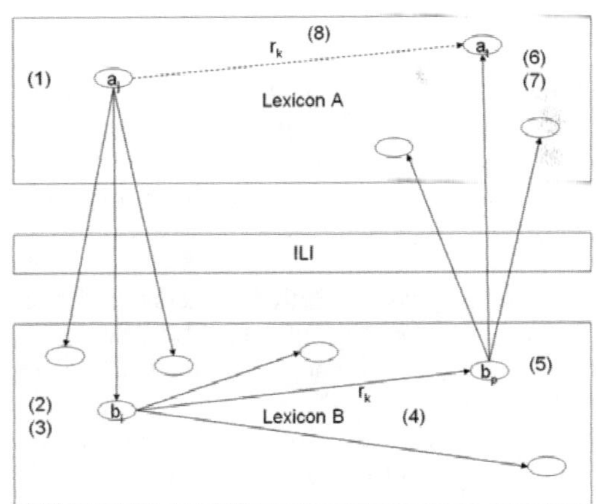

Figure 5. Finding New Relations.

Every local wordnet has to provide a web service API with the following methods:

1. GetWeightedSynsetsByIli(ILIid, ILIversion)
2. GetSynsetById(sysnsetID)
3. GetSynsetsByLemma(lemma)

[1] For example, the Chinese and the Italian wordnets considered as our case-study use respectively versions 1.6 and 1.5.

[2] It should be noted, however, that the conversion between different WN versions could not be accurate so the mapping is always proposed with a probability score.

The returned synsets of each method must be formatted in XML following the schema depicted in Figure 6:

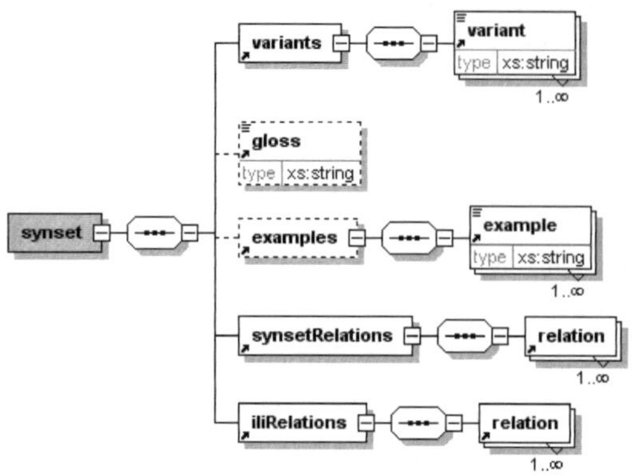

Figure 6. Schema of Wordnet Synsets Returned by WN Web Services.

The scores returned by the method "GetWeightedSynsetsByIli" are used by our module to calculate the reliability rating for each new proposed relation.

3.3 A Case Study: Cross-fertilization between Italian and Chinese Wordnets.

We explore this idea with a case-study involving the ItalianWordNet (Roventini et al., 2003) and the Academia Sinica Bilingual Ontological Wordnet (Sinica BOW, Huang et al., 2004).

The BOW integrates three resources: WordNet, English-Chinese Translation Equivalents Database (ECTED), and SUMO (Suggested Upper Merged Ontology). With the integration of these three key resources, Sinica BOW functions both as an English-Chinese bilingual wordnet and a bilingual lexical access to SUMO. Sinica Bow currently has two bilingual versions, corresponding to WordNet 1.6. and 1.7. Based on these bootstrapped versions, a Chinese Wordnet (CWN, Huang et al. 2005) is under construction with handcrafted senses and lexical semantic relations. For the current experiment, we have used the version linking to WordNet 1.6.

ItalWordNet was realized as an extension of the Italian component of EuroWordNet. It comprises a general component consisting of about 50,000 synsets and terminological wordnets linked to the generic wordnet by means of a specific set of relations. Each synset of ItalWordNet is linked to the Interlingual-Index (ILI).

The two lexicons refer to different versions of the ILI (1.5 for IWN and 1.6 for BOW), thus making it necessary to provide a mapping between the two versions. On the other hand, no mapping is necessary for the set of synset relations used, since both of them adopt the same set.

For the purposes of evaluating the cross-lingual module, we have developed two web-services for managing a subset of the two resources.

The following Figure shows a very simple example where our procedure discovers and proposes a new meronymy relation for the Italian synset {passaggio,strada,via}. This synset is equivalent to the ILI "road,route" that is ILI-connected with BOW synset "道路,道 ,路" (dao_lu, dao, lu) (Figure 7, A) . The Chinese synset has a meronymy relation with the synset "十字路口" (wan) (B). This last synset is equivalent to the ILI "bend, crook, turn" that is ILI-connected with Italian WordNet synset "curvatura, svolta, curva" (C). Therefore the procedure will propose a new candidate meronymy relation between the two Italian WordNet synsets (D).

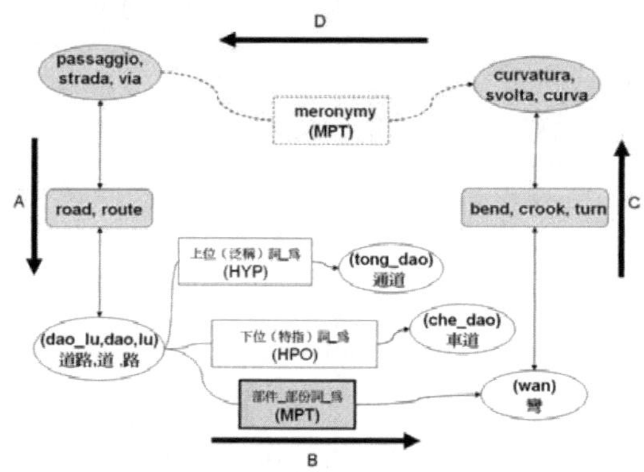

Figure 7. Example of a New Proposed Meronymy Relation for Italian.

3.4 Considerations and Lessons Learned

Given the diversity of the languages for which wordnets exist, we note that it is difficult to implement an operational standard across all typologically different languages. Work on enriching and merging multilingual resources presupposes that the resources involved are all encoded with the same standard. However, even with the best efforts of the NLP community, there are only a small number of language resources encoded in any given standard. In the current work, we presuppose a de-facto standard, i.e. a shared and conventionalized architecture, the WordNet one. Since the WordNet framework is both conventionalized and widely followed, our system is able to rely on it without resorting to a more substantial and comprehensive standard. In the case, for instance, of integration of lexicons with different underlying linguistic models, the availability of the MILE (Calzolari et al., 2003) was an essential prerequisite of our work. Nevertheless, even from the perspective of the same model, a certain degree of standardization is required, at least at the format level.

From a more general point of view, and even from the perspective of a limited experiment such as the one described in this paper, we must note that the realization of the new vision of distributed and interoperable language resources is strictly intertwined with at least two prerequisites. On the one side, the language resources need to be available over the web; on the other, the language resource community will have to reconsider current distribution policies, and to investigate the possibility of developing an "Open Source" concept for LRs.

4 Conclusion

Our proposal to make distributed wordnets inter-operable has the following applications in processing of lexical resources:

- Enriching existing resources: information is often not complete in any given wordnet: by making two wordnets inter-operable, we can bootstrap semantic relations and other information from other wordnets.
- Creation of new resources: multilingual lexicons can be bootstrapped by linking different language wordnets through ILI.
- Validation of existing resources: semantic relation information and other synset assignments can be validated when it is re-inforced by data from a different wordnet.

In particular, our work can be proposed as a prototype of a web application that would support the Global WordNet Grid initiative (www.globalwordnet.org/gwa/gwa_grid.htm).

Any multilingual process, such as cross-lingual information retrieval, must involve both resources and tools in a specific language and language pairs. For instance, a multilingual query given in Italian but intended for querying English, Chinese, French, German, and Russian texts, can be send to five different nodes on the Grid for query expansion, as well as performing the query itself. In this way, language specific query techniques can be applied in parallel to achieve best results that can be integrated in the future. As multilingualism clearly becomes one of the major challenges of the future of web-based knowledge engineering, WordNet emerges as one leading candidate for a shared platform for representing a lexical knowledge model for different languages of the world. This is true even if it has to be recognized that the wordnet model is lacking in some important semantic information (like, for instance, a way to represent the semantic predicate). However, such knowledge and resources are distributed. In order to create a shared multi-lingual knowledge base for cross-lingual processing based on these distributed resources, an initiative to create a grid-like structure has been recently proposed and promoted by the Global WordNet Association, but until now has remained a wishful thinking. The success of this initiative will depend on whether there will be tools to access and manipulate the rich internal semantic structure of distributed multi-lingual WordNets. We believe that our work on LeXFlow offers such a tool to provide inter-operable web-services to access distributed multilingual WordNets on the grid.

This allows us to exploit in a cross-lingual framework the wealth of monolingual lexical information built in the last decade.

5 References

Nicoletta Calzolari, Francesca Bertagna, Alessandro Lenci and Monica Monachini, editors. 2003. *Standards and Best Practice for Multilingual Computational Lexicons. MILE (the Multilingual ISLE Lexical Entry)*. ISLE CLWG Deliverable D2.2 & 3.2. Pisa.

Nicoletta Calzolari and Claudia Soria. 2005. A New Paradigm for an Open Distributed Language Resource Infrastructure: the Case of Computational Lexicons. In *Proceedings of the AAAI Spring Symposium "Knowledge Collection from Volunteer Contributors (KCVC05)"*, pages 110-114, Stanford, CA.

Nicoletta Calzolari. 2006. Technical and Strategic issues on Language Resources for a Research Infrastructure In *Proceedings of the International Symposium on Large-scale Knowledge Resources* (LKR2006), pages 53-58, Tokyo, Tokyo Institute of Technology.

Jordi Daudé, Lluis Padró and German Rigau. 2001. A Complete WN1.5 to WN1.6 Mapping. In *Proceedings of NAACL Workshop "WordNet and Other Lexical Resources: Applications, Extensions and*

Customizations", pages 83-88, Pittsburg, PA, USA, Association for Computational Linguistics.

Greg Gulrajani and David Harrison. 2002. SHAWEL: Sharable and Interactive Web-Lexicons. In *Proceedings of the LREC2002 Workshop on Tools and Resources in Field Linguistics*, pages 1-4, Las Palmas, Canary Islands, Spain.

Chu-Ren Huang, Ru-Yng Chang, and Shiang-Bin Lee. 2004. Sinica BOW (Bilingual Ontological Wordnet): Integration of Bilingual WordNet and SUMO. In *Proceedings of LREC2004*, pages 1553-1556, Lisbon, Portugal.

Chu-Ren Huang, Chun-Ling Chen, Cui-Xia Weng, Hsiang-Ping Lee, Yong-Xiang Chen and Keh-jiann Chen. 2005. The Sinica Sense Management System: Design and Implementation. *Computational Linguistics and Chinese Language Processing.* 10(4): 417-430.

Marc Kemps-Snijders, Mark-Jan Nederhof, and Peter Wittenburg. 2006. LEXUS, a web-based tool for manipulating lexical resources. Accepted for publication in *Proceedings of LREC2006*, Genoa, Italy.

Andrea Marchetti, Maurizio Tesconi, and Salvatore Minutoli. 2005. XFlow: An XML-Based Document-Centric Workflow. In *Proceedings of WISE'05*, pages 290-303, New York, NY, USA.

Wim Peters, Piek Vossen, Pedro Diez-Orzas, and Geert Adriaens. 1998. Cross-linguistic Alignment of Wordnets with an Inter-Lingual-Index. In Nancy Ide, Daniel Greenstein, and Piek Vossen, editors, Special Issue on EuroWordNet, *Computers and the Humanities*, 32(2-3): 221-251.

Laurent Romary, Gil Francopoulo, Monica Monachini, and Susanne Salmon-Alt 2006. Lexical Markup Framework (LMF): working to reach a consensual ISO standard on lexicons. Accepted for publication in *Proceedings of LREC2006*, Genoa, Italy.

Adriana Roventini, Antonietta Alonge, Francesca Bertagna, Nicoletta Calzolari, Christian Girardi, Bernardo Magnini, Rita Marinelli, and Antonio Zampolli. 2003. ItalWordNet: Building a Large Semantic Database for the Automatic Treatment of Italian. In Antonio Zampolli, Nicoletta Calzolari, and Laura Cignoni, editors, *Computational Linguistics in Pisa*, IEPI, Pisa-Roma, pages 745-791.

Nilda Ruimy, Monica Monachini, Elisabetta Gola, Nicoletta Calzolari, Cristina Del Fiorentino, Marisa Ulivieri, and Sergio Rossi. 2003. A Computational Semantic Lexicon of Italian: SIMPLE. In Antonio Zampolli, Nicoletta Calzolari, and Laura Cignoni, editors, *Computational Linguistics in Pisa*, IEPI, Pisa-Roma, pages 821-864.

Claudia Soria, Maurizio Tesconi, Francesca Bertagna, Nicoletta Calzolari, Andrea Marchetti, and Monica Monachini. 2006. Moving to Dynamic Computational Lexicons with LeXFlow. Accepted for publication in *Proceedings of LREC2006*, Genova, Italy.

Piek Vossen. 1998. Introduction to EuroWordNet. In Nancy Ide, Daniel Greenstein, and Piek Vossen, editors, Special Issue on EuroWordNet, *Computers and the Humanities*, 32(2-3): 73-89.

The LexALP Information System: Term Bank and Corpus for Multilingual Legal Terminology Consolidated

Verena Lyding, Elena Chiocchetti
EURAC research
Viale Druso 1, 39100 Bozen/Bolzano - Italy
forename.name@eurac.edu

Gilles Sérasset, Francis Brunet-Manquat
GETA-CLIPS IMAG
BP 53, 38041 Grenoble cedex 9 - France
forename.name@imag.fr

Abstract

Standard techniques used in multilingual terminology management fail to describe legal terminologies as they are bound to different legal systems and terms do not share a common meaning. In the LexALP project, we use a technique defined for general lexical databases to achieve cross language interoperability between languages of the Alpine Convention. In this paper we present the methodology and tools developed for the collection, description and harmonisation of the legal terminology of spatial planning and sustainable development in the four languages of the countries of the Alpine Space.

1 Introduction

The aim of the LexALP project is to harmonise the terminology used by the Alpine Convention, both for internal purposes and for communication among the member states. The Alpine Convention is an international treaty signed by all states of the Alpine territory (France, Monaco, Switzerland Liechtenstein, Austria, Germany, Italy and Slovenia) for the protection of landscape and sustainable development of this mountain area[1]. The member states speak four different languages, namely French, German, Italian, and Slovene and have different legal systems and traditions.

Hence arises the need for a systematization and uniformation of terminology and clear translation equivalence in all four languages. For this reason, the project intends to provide all stakeholders and the wider public with an information system which combines three main components, a terminology data base, a multilingual corpus and the relative bibliographic data base. In this way the manually revised, elaborated and validated (harmonised) quadrilingual information on the legal terminology (i.e. complete terminological entries) will be closely interacting with a facility to dynamically search for additional contexts in a relevant set of legal texts in all languages and for all main legal systems involved.

2 Multilingual legal information system

The information system for the terminology of the Alpine Convention, with a specific focus on spatial planning and sustainable development, will give the possibility to search for relevant terms and their (harmonised or rejected) translations in all 4 official languages of the Alpine Convention in the first module, the term bank. Next to retrieving synonyms and translation equivalents within each legal system, the user will be provided with a representative context and a valid definition of the concept under consideration. Source information will be provided for each text field in the terminological entry.

Via a link from the terminological data base to the second module, the corpus facility, the information system will give the possibility to search the corpus for further contexts.

Finally, both term bank and corpus will be interacting with a third module, the bibliographic database, so as to allow retrieving full information on text excepts cited in the term bank and to store important meta data on corpus documents.

[1] cf. also http: www.alpenkonvention.org

Proceedings of the Workshop on Multilingual Language Resources and Interoperability, pages 25–31,
Sydney, July 2006.

3 Terminological data

3.1 Data categories and motivations

The data categories present in the terminology database allow entering and organising relevant information on the concept under analysis. The term bank interface allows entering of the following terminological data categories: denomination/term, definition, context, note, sources (text fields), grammatical information to the term, harmonisation status, processing status, geographical usage, frequency and domain, according to the appositely elaborated domain classification structure[2] (pull down menus). Again by means of pull-down menus the terminologist will be able to signal to the users which terms are already processed (i.e. checked by legal experts), harmonised or rejected and - most important - to which legal system they belong (the menu geographical usage allows to specify this information). Furthermore it is possible to specify synonyms, short forms, abbreviations etc. in the terminological entry and, if necessary, link them to the relative full information already present in the term bank (however, no direct access to these linked data is possible, this must be done via the search interface). Finally, the terminologist is given the possibility of writing general comments to the entry. At the very end of one language entry the terminologist can decide whether to release the data to the public (by clicking on the button 'finish') or keep it for further finetuning (button 'update').

Each term is created in its 'language volume' and described by means of all necessary information. As soon as one or all equivalents in the other languages are available too, the single entries can be linked to each other with the help of an axie (see detailed description below).

Searches can be done for all languages or on a user-defined selection of source and target languages. Presently the database allows global searching in all text fields and filtering by source, author, date of creation, as well as by axie name and ids. Results can be displayed in full form, as a short list of terms only or in XML. Some export/import functions are granted.

As the term bank serves mainly the scope of diffusing harmonised terminology, the four translation equivalents (validated by a group of experts) are displayed together, whereas rejected synonyms are displayed separately for each search language. In this way the user may well look for a non validated synonym and find it in the database but be warned as to which is the preferred term and its harmonised equivalents in the other languages. Figure 1 shows such a situation where the French rejected term "transport intra-alpin" is linked to the harmonised term "trafic intra-alpin".

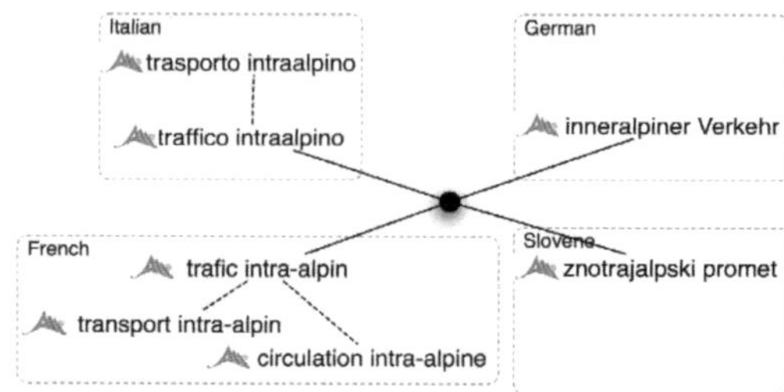

Figure 1: A set of Alpine Convention terms and their relations

3.2 Monolingual data

The LexALP term bank consists in 5 volumes for French, German, Italian, Slovene and English (no data is being entered for this fifth language at the moment), which contain the term descriptions. The set of data categories is represented in an XML structure that follows a common schema.

```
<entry id="fra.trafic_intra-alpin.1010743.e"
       lang="fra"
       legalSystem="AC"
       process_status="FINALISED"
       status="HARMONISED">
  <term>trafic intra-alpin</term>
  <grammar>n.m.</grammar>
  <domain>Transport</domain>
  <usage frequency="common"
         geographical-code="INT"
         technical="false"/>
  <relatedTerm
    isHarmonised="false"
    relationToTerm="Synonym"
    termref="fra.transport_intra-alpin…"/>
  <relatedTerm
    isHarmonised="false"
    relationToTerm="Synonym"
    termref="fra.circulation_intra-…"/>
  <definition>
    [T]rafic constitué de trajets ayant leur
    point de départ et/ou d'arrivée à
    l'intérieur de l'espace alpin.
  </definition>
  <source>Prot. Transp., art. 2 </source>
  <context url="http://www...">
    Des projets routiers à grand débit pour
    le trafic intra-alpin peuvent être
    réalisés, si [...].
  </context>
</entry>
```

Figure 2: XML form of the term 'trafic intra-alpin'

Each entry represents a unique term/meaning. Terms with the same denomination, but belong-

[2] See also 4.1

ing to different legal systems have, de facto, different meanings. Hence, different entries are created. Terms with different denominations but conveying the same 'meaning' (concept) are also represented using different entries[3]. In this case, the entries are linked through a synonymy relation.

Figure 2 shows the XML structure of the French term "trafic intra-alpin", as defined in the Alpine Convention. The term entry is associated to a unique identifier used to establish relations between volume entries.

The example term belongs to the Alpine Convention legal system[4] (code `AC`). The entry also bears the information on its status (harmonised or rejected) and its processing status (to be processed, provisionally processed or finalised).

In addition, a definition (along with its source) and a context may be given. The definition and context should be extracted from a legal text, which must be identified in the source field.

3.3 Achieving language/legal system interoperability

As the project deals with several different legal terms, standard techniques used in multilingual terminology management need to be adapted to the peculiarities of the specialised language of the law. Indeed, terms in different languages are (generally) defined according to different legal systems and these legal systems cannot be changed. Hence, it is not possible to define a common 'meaning' that could be used as a pivot for language interoperability[5]. In this respect, legal terminology is closer to general lexicography than to standard terminology.

In order to achieve language/legal system interoperability we had several options that are used in general lexicography.

Using a set of bilingual dictionaries is not an option here, as we have to deal with at least 16 language/legal system couples (with alpine Convention and EU levels, but without taking into account regional levels). Moreover, such a solution will not reflect the multilingual aspect of the Alpine Convention or the Swiss legal system. Finally, building bilingual volumes between the French and Italian legal systems is far beyond the objectives of the LexALP project.

Another solution would be to use an "Eurowordnet like" approach (Vossen, 1998) where a specific language/legal system is used as a pivot and elements of the other systems are linked by equivalent or near-equivalent links. As such an approach artificially puts a language in the pivot position, it generally leads to an "ethnocentric" view of the other languages. The advantage being that the architecture uses the bilingual competence of lexicographers to achieve multilingualism.

In this project, we chose to use 'interlingual acceptions' (a.k.a. axies) as defined in (Sérasset, 1994) to represent such complex contrastive phenomena as generally described in general lexicography work. In this approach, each 'term meaning' is associated to an interlingual acception (or axie). These axies are used to achieve interoperability as a pivot linking terms of different languages bearing the same meaning.

However, as we are dealing with legal terms (bound to different legal systems), it is generally not possible to find terms in different languages that bear the same meaning. In fact such terms can only be found in the Alpine Convention (which is considered as a legal system expressed in all the considered languages). Hence, we use these terms to achieve interoperability between languages. In this aspect, we are close to Eurowordnet's approach as we use a specific legal system as a pivot, but in our case the pivot itself is generally a quadrilingual set of entries.

These harmonised Alpine Convention terms are linked through an interlingual acception. An axie is a place holder for relations. Each interlingual acception may be linked to several term entries in the languages volumes through `termref` elements and to other interlingual acceptions through `axieref` elements, as illustrated in Figure 3.

```
<axie id="axi..1011424.e">
 <termref
  idref="ita.traffico_intraalpino.1010654.e"
  lang="ita"/>
 <termref
  idref="fra.trafic_intra-alpin.1010743.e"
  lang="fra"/>
 <termref
  idref="deu.inneralpiner_Verkehr.1011065.e"
```

[3] Variants, acronyms, etc. are not considered as different denominations.

[4] Strictly speaking, the Alpine Convention does not constitute a legal system per se.

[5] Consider for instance the difference between the Italian and the Austrian concepts of journalists' professional confidentiality. Whereas the *Redaktionsgeheimnis* explicitly underlines that the journalist can refuse to witness in court in order to keep the professional secret, in Italy the *segreto giornalistico* must obligatorily be lifted on a judge's request. The two concepts have overlapping meanings in the two states, however, they diverge greatly with respect to the behaviour in court.

```
  lang="deu"/>
 <termref
  idref="slo.znotrajalpski_promet.1011132.e"
  lang="slo"/>
 <axieref idref=""/>
 <misc></misc>
</axie>
```

Figure 3: XML form of the interlingual acception illustrated Figure 1

The `termref` relation establishes a direct translation relation between these harmonised equivalents. Then, national legal terms are indirectly linked to Alpine Convention terms through the `axieref` relation as illustrated in Figure 4.

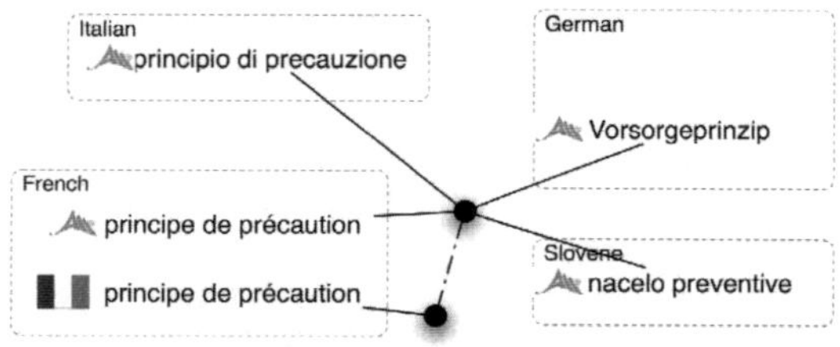

Figure 4: An example French term, linked to a quadrilingual Alpine Convention Term.

4 Corpus

4.1 Corpus content

The corpus comprises around 3000 legal documents of eight legal systems (Germany, Italy, France, Switzerland, Austria, Slovenia, European law and international law with the specific framework of the Alpine Convention,) (see table 1).

AT	CH	DE	FR	IT	SI	AC	EU	INT
612	119	62	613	490	213	38	791	149

Table 1: Corpus documents for each legal system

Documents of the supranational level are provided in up to four languages (subject to availability). National legislation is generally added in the national language (monolingual documents) and in case of Switzerland (multilingual documents) in the three official languages of that nation (French, German and Italian).

The documents are selected by legal experts of the respective legal systems following predefined criteria:

- entire documents (no single paragraphs or excerpts etc.);
- strong relevance to the subjects 'spatial planning and sustainable development' as described in art. 9 of the relative Alpine Convention Protocol;
- primary sources of the law for every system at national and international/EU level, i.e. normative texts only (laws, codes etc.);
- latest amendments and versions of all legislation (at time of collection: June – August 2005);
- terminological relevance.

Each document is classified according to the following (bibliographical) categories: full title, short title, abbreviation, legal system, language, legal hierarchy, legal text type, subfield (1, 2 and 3), official date, official number, published in official journal (date, number, page), … The bibliographical information of all documents is stored in a database and can at any time be consulted by the user.

The subfields have been elaborated and selected by a team of legal experts, taking into account the classification specificities followed by the Alpine Convention and the need to classify texts from several different legal systems according to one common structure. For this reason, the legal experts have subdivided the fields spatial planning and sustainable development into 5 main areas, in accordance with the Alpine Convention Protocol dealing with these subjects and subsequently adopted an EU-based model for further subdividing the 5 main topics in such a way that all countries involved could classify their selected documents under a maximum of 3 main items, the first of which must be indicated obligatorily. This classification allows an easy selection of all subsets of documents according to subject field.

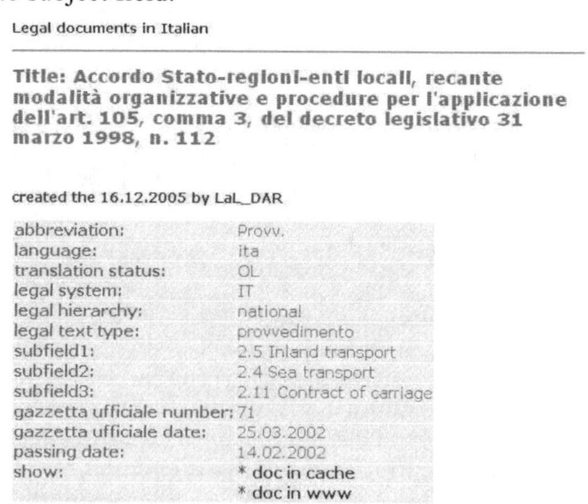
Legal documents in Italian

Title: Accordo Stato-regioni-enti locali, recante modalità organizzative e procedure per l'applicazione dell'art. 105, comma 3, del decreto legislativo 31 marzo 1998, n. 112

created the 16.12.2005 by LaL_DAR

abbreviation:	Provv.
language:	ita
translation status:	OL
legal system:	IT
legal hierarchy:	national
legal text type:	provvedimento
subfield1:	2.5 Inland transport
subfield2:	2.4 Sea transport
subfield3:	2.11 Contract of carriage
gazzetta ufficiale number:	71
gazzetta ufficiale date:	25.03.2002
passing date:	14.02.2002
show:	* doc in cache * doc in www

Figure 5: Example of document classification

```
<header
 lang="ita"
 creator="X"
 created="Fri Feb 17 10:45:15 CET 2006">
<h.title>
 Legge_regionale_25974.14_87.txt
</h.title>
<bibID>
 17658
</bibID>
</header>
```

Figure 6: XML-header of corpus documents

```
<text id="17658">
<body id="17658.b">
  <div type="intro" id="17658.b.i">
    <p id="17658.b.i.p1">
      <title id="17658.b.i.p1.ti1">
        LEGGE REGIONALE 15/05/1987, N. 014
        Disciplina dell' esercizio [...] di
        fauna selvatica.
      </title>
    </p>
  </div>
  <div type="section" id="17658.b.c0.se1">
    <p id="17658.b.c0.se1.p1">
      <title id="17658.b.c0.se1.p1.ti1">
        Art. 1
      </title>
    </p>
    <p id="17658.b.c0.se1.p2">
      <s id="17658.b.c0.se1.p2.s1">
        1. Sull' intero territorio
        regionale la caccia selettiva
        per qualita', [...]
      </s>
      <s id="17658.b.c0.se1.p2.s2">
        a) capriolo: dal 15 maggio al
         15 gennaio;
      </s>
      <s id="17658.b.c0.se1.p2.s3">
        b) cinghiale: dal 15 giugno
        al 15 gennaio;
      </s>
    </p>
    <p id="17658.b.c0.se1.p3">
      <s id="17658.b.c0.se1.p3.s1">
        2. E' ammesso l' uso [...]
      </s>
    </p>
  </div>
</body>
</text>
```

Figure 7: XML-structure of corpus document

4.2 Structural organization of corpus data

Collected in raw text format (one file for each legal text) the documents are first transformed into XML-structured files and in a second step inserted into the database.

The XML-annotation is done in compliance with the Corpus Encoding Standard for XML (XCES) [6]. Slightly simplified, the provided schema[7] serves to add structural information to the documents. Each text is segmented into subsections like: preamble, chapter, section, paragraph, title and sentence. Furthermore, a link to the classification data (bibliographic data base) is inserted and, in case of multilingual documents, alignment is done at sentence level.

The XML-annotated documents hold all the information needed for the insertion into the corpus database, such as structural mark-up and bibliographical information. The full text documents are transformed into sets of database entries, which can be imported into the database.

4.3 Technical organization of corpus data

Following the *bistro* approach as realized for the Corpus Ladin dl'Eurac (CLE) (Streiter et al. 2004) the corpus data is stored in a relational database (PostgreSQL). The information present in the XML-annotated documents is distributed among four main tables: document_info, corpus_words, corpus_structure, corpus_alignment.

The four tables can be described as follows:

document_info: This table holds the meta-information about the documents; each category (like full title, short title, abbreviation, legal system, language, etc.) is represented by a separate column. For each legal document one entry (one row) with unique identification number is added to the table. These identification numbers are cited in the XML-header of the corpus documents.

corpus_words: This table holds the actual text of the collected documents. Instead of storing entire paragraphs as it was done during the creation of CLE, for this corpus a different approach is being tested. Every annotated text is split into an indexed sequence of words, starting with counter one. Once inserted into the database a text is stored as a set of tuples composed of word, position in text and document id (as a reference to the document information).

corpus_structure: This table holds all information about the internal structure of the documents. Titles, sentences, paragraphs etc. are stored by indicating starting and ending point of the section. For each segment a tuple of segment type, segment id, starting point (indicated by the index of the first word), ending point (indicated by the index of the last word) and document id is added.

corpus_alignment: This table defines the alignment of multilingual documents. By providing one column for each language the texts are aligned via the document ids or via the ids of single segments.

[6] http://www.cs.vassar.edu/XCES/

[7] http://www.cs.vassar.edu/XCES/schema/xcesDoc.xsd

The tables are interconnected by explicitly stated references. That means that the columns of one table refer to the values of a certain column of another table. As shown in figure 8 all tables hold a column *document_id* that refers to the document id of the table document_info. Furthermore, the table corpus_structure holds references to the column *position* of the table corpus_words.

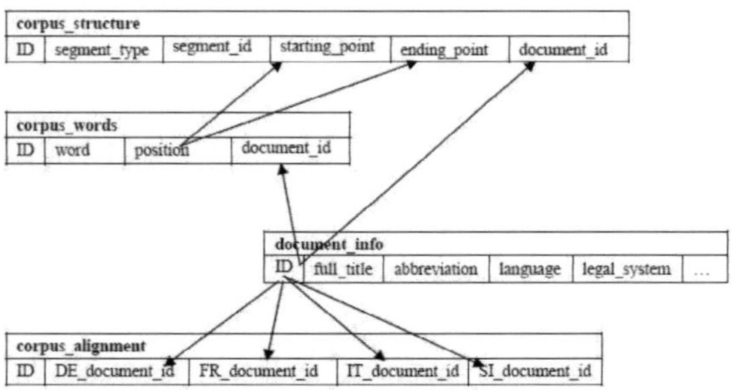

Figure 8: Interconnection of tables

5 Searching the corpus

Due to the fine-grained classification (see section 4.1) and the structural mark-up (see section 4.2) of all corpus documents, corpus searches can be restricted in the following ways:

- by specifying a subset of corpus documents over which the search should be carried out (e.g. all documents of legal system CH with language French);
- by choosing the type of unit to be displayed (whole paragraphs <p>, sentences <s>, titles <title>, …);
- by searching for whole words only (exact match) or parts of words (fuzzy match);
- by restricting the number of hits to be displayed at a time.

For searches in multilingual documents it will be possible to search for aligned segments, specifying search word as well as target translation. For example, the user could search for all alignments of German-Italian sentences that contain the word *Umweltschutz* translated as *tutela ambientale* (and not with *protezione dell'ambiente*).
Figure 9 shows a simple interface for searching monolingual documents.

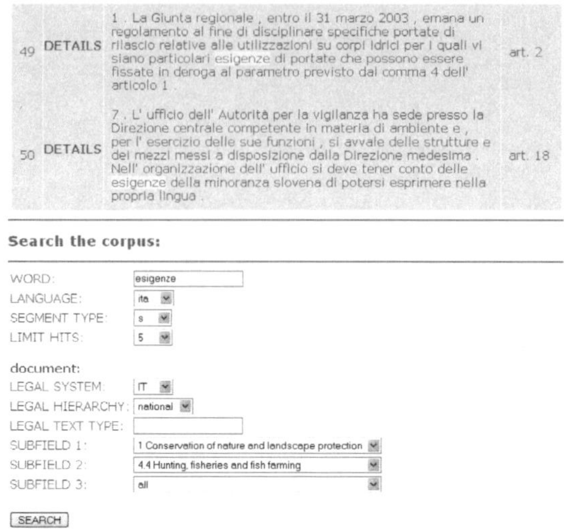

Figure 9: Example search over monolingual documents

6 Interaction term bank and corpus

Term bank and corpus are independent components which together form the LexALP Information System.

The interaction between corpus and term bank will concern in particular 1) corpus segments used as contexts and definitions in the terminological entries, 2) short source references in the term bank (and the associated sets of bibliographical information) and 3) legal terms.

6.1 Entering data into term bank

When adding citations to a term bank entry, the relative bibliographic information will automatically be counterchecked with the contents of the bibliographical database. In case the information about the cited document is already present in the DB, a link to the term bank can be added. Otherwise the terminologist is asked to provide all information about the new source to the bibliographic database and later create the link.

Next to static contexts and definitions present for each terminological entry, each entry will show a button for the dynamic creation of contexts. Hitting the button will start a context search in the corpus and return all sentences containing the term under consideration.

6.2 Searching the corpus

When searching the corpus the user will have the opportunity to highlight terms present in the term bank. In the same way standardised or rejected terms can be brought out. Via a link it will then be possible to directly access the term bank entry for the term found in the corpus.

In general each corpus segment is linked to the full set of bibliographic information of the document that the segment is part of. Accessing the source information will lead the user to a detailed overview as shown in figure 4.

7 Conclusion

In this paper, we have presented the LexALP information system, used to collect, describe and harmonise the terminology used by the Alpine Convention and to link it with national legal terminology of the alpine Convention's member states. Even if we currently give a specific focus on spatial planning and sustainable development, the project is not restricted to these fields and the methodology and tools developed can be adapted to legal terminology of other fields.

In this paper we also proposed a solution to the encoding of multilingual legal terminologies in a context where standard techniques used in multilingual terminology management usually fail.

The terminology developed and the corpus used for its development will be accessible online for the stakeholders and the wider public through the LexALP information system.

Acknowledgements

The LexALP research project started in January 2005 thanks to the funds granted by the INTERREG IIIB "Alpine Space" Programme, a Community Initiative Programme funded by the European Regional Development Fund.

References

Gilles Sérasset. 1994. *Interlingual Lexical Organisation for Multilingual Lexical Databases in NADIA.* In Makoto Nagao, editor, COLING-94, volume 1, pages 278—282, August.

Streiter, O., Stuflesser, M. & Ties, I. (2004). CLE, an aligned Tri-lingual Ladin-Italian-German Corpus. Corpus Design and Interface, *LREC 2004, Workshop on "First Steps for Language Documentation of Minority Languages: Computational Linguistic Tools for Morphology, Lexicon and Corpus Compilation"* Lisbon, May 24, 2004.

Vossen, Piek. 1998. Introduction to EuroWordNet. In Nancy Ide, Daniel Greenstein, and Piek Vossen, editors, Special Issue on EuroWordNet, *Computers and the Humanities*, 32(2-3): 73-89.

Wright, Sue Ellen 2001. *Data Categories for Terminology Management.* In Sue Ellen Wright & Gerhard Budin, editors, Handbook of Terminology Management, volume 2, pages 552-569.

The Development of a Multilingual Collocation Dictionary

Sylviane Cardey
Centre Tesnière
Université de Franche-Comté
France
sylviane.cardey@univ-fcomte.fr

Rosita Chan
Centre Tesnière
&
University of Panama
chan.rosita@hotmail.com

Peter Greenfield
Centre Tesnière
Université de Franche-Comté
France
peter.greenfield@univ-fcomte.fr

Abstract

In this paper we discuss the development of a multilingual collocation dictionary for translation purposes. By 'collocation' we mean not only set or fixed expressions including idioms, simple co-occurrences of items and metaphorical uses, but also translators' paraphrases. We approach this problem from two directions. Firstly we identify certain linguistic phenomena and lexicographical requirements that need to be respected in the development of such dictionaries. The second and other direction concerns the development of such dictionaries in which linguistic phenomena and lexicographic attributes are themselves a means of access to the collocations. The linguistic phenomena and lexicographical requirements concern variously placing the sense of collocations rather than headwords or other access methods at the centre of interest, together with collocation synonymy and translation equivalence, polysemy and non-reversibility of the lexis, and other more lexicographic properties such as varieties of language and regionalisms, and types of translation.

1 Introduction

In work with developing multilingual collocation based dictionaries for translation purposes across a wide variety of domains (Cardey and Greenfield, 1999; Chan 2005) various interesting linguistic phenomena and lexicographic requirements have been observed. In the context of such dictionaries, by the term collocation we include not only set or fixed expressions (Moon, 1995, Tables 1.1 and 1.2, pp.19-20) including idioms, simple co-occurrences of items (*plane ticket*) and metaphorical uses (*spill the beans*), but also, as we will show, translators' paraphrases where these are needed. Linguistic phenomena include ones concerning sense (for example synonymy and translation equivalence, polysemy and non-reversibility). Lexicographical requirements include for example the requirement (for consistency purposes amongst others) that the collocation (as article) be the centre of interest rather than the headword(s) whose role is one of access to the collocations. This is principally because the object of such dictionaries should be based on inter-lingual collocation sense group correspondence, translation of headwords being essentially incidental. Another way to view this is that if what we wish to model is a dictionary of senses, these senses are expressed by interpretations in the form of collocations. However, difficulties are engendered with this approach. For example, headwords are typically canonical in form whilst their corresponding lexical units in collocations can be variants (for example inflected or be derivations). Furthermore, in reality the definition of a collocation structure for lexicographic purposes can itself be complex, for example to cater for or indicate information such as inflected forms, synonymy and translation equivalence, grammatical labelling and comments (Gaveiro, 1998, pp. 26 - 27, 64 - 65).

More recently, our interest has been concerned with how to develop such multilingual collocation dictionaries including access to collocations based on linguistic phenomena as well as by headwords (a headword can only be a single word, even for idioms) (Chan, 2005) where the issues of particular cases at the semantic level and at the grammatical level are important. Here

Proceedings of the Workshop on Multilingual Language Resources and Interoperability, pages 32–39,
Sydney, July 2006.

the access to collocations can be by posing a problem; one can ask for those collocations which present a problem of article for example.

The linguistic phenomena and lexicographic requirements are ones that are candidates for modelling such dictionaries using formal methods, for example using the Z formal specification language (Spivey, 1992), the impetus being that certain domains in which such dictionaries are used are safety critical in nature. This has resulted in work in respect of the state invariants peculiar to specialised multilingual collocation based dictionaries (Greenfield, 1998a; Greenfield, 1998b).

In response to these various observed linguistic phenomena and lexicographical requirements, the MultiCoDiCT (Multilingual Collocation Dictionary System Centre Tesnière) system was developed as a research aid tool for multilingual lexicographic research (Greenfield et al., 1999; Greenfield, 2003). The basic model underpinning MultiCoDiCT dictionaries reposes on the concept of the collocation sense group as a means to ensure integrity and consistent access to the collocations. In this model a collocation in a language appears only once, whereas in conventional dictionary models it is the headword in a language that appears only once. This constraint leads us to generality; not only do we obtain reversibility of translation with no extra effort, we obtain non-reversibility of the lexis where this happens to be the case. Furthermore, headword access to a collocation also provides direct access to the other collocations in the dictionary with an equivalent sense (or senses for polysemic collocations).

More recently, work on linguistic phenomena and lexicographic attributes based access to collocations (as well as headword access) has resulted in a prototype system using an algorithmic approach (Chan, 2005) using the Studygram system (Cardey and Greenfield, 1992).

In the paper we first review the linguistic phenomena and lexicographic requirements that we have discerned for such multilingual collocation dictionaries. We then discuss the development of such dictionaries in which the linguistic phenomena and lexicographic attributes are themselves a means of access to the collocations. Finally, in the conclusion we show how Studygram and MultiCoDiCT can be integrated in order to provide a more general approach for the access to such multilingual collocation dictionaries.

2 Linguistic phenomena and lexicographic requirements

In the context of lexicographical research, collocations as articles in multilingual dictionaries present various linguistic phenomena and lexicographic requirements which are sufficiently generic but also sufficiently important lexicographically as to warrant some generalised support. The various phenomena and requirements are illustrated in this section by the essentially traditional headword access method to collocations as provided by the MultiCoDiCT system.

The linguistic phenomena concern synonymy, polysemy and non-reversibility of the lexis in translation. For example synonymy is indicated by more than one collocation having the same sense equivalence variously in the source language or in the target language (in the illustrations that follow the source language is on the left and the target language is on the right); see Figures 1 and 2.

Spanish	**French**
Headword	
boleto	billet
Collocations	
billete de avión (Spain) boleto de avión (Americanism)	billet d'avion

Figure 1. Synonymy in the source language

French	**Spanish**
Headword	
billet	billete(Spain) boleto(Americanism)
Collocations	
billet d'avion	billete de avión (Spain) boleto de avión (Americanism)

Figure 2. Synonymy in the target language

In the above two examples, the Spanish collocations include annotations indicating regionalisms such as *(Spain)* (Chan, 1999). We say that collocations in the same or different languages which are equivalent in that they have the same sense are members of the same *sense group*. In the above examples we can also observe various lexicographical requirements such as headwords and the use of structured annotations to display the regionalism information.

Polysemy is indicated by the presence of translations with different senses, that is, where a collocation is the member of more than one sense group. The example that we use is drawn from an archtypical bilingual dictionary (Werthe-Hengsanga, 2001) of Thai-French image expressions in the zoological domain with the particularity that the types of translation are shown by lexicographic annotations as follows:

- Eq equivalent – supplied, provided that an equivalent can be found
- LT literal translation – word for word
- AS analytical sense – literal translation reformulated in correct French
- FS functional sense – the true sense of the translated collocation

The Thai is shown here by means of a phonetic transcription using ASCII characters (which in fact does not provide an adequate cover but this matter is not pursued here). An example of a polysemic Thai collocation with 3 functional senses (FS) is shown in Figure 3.

Thai	French
Headword	
hmu:	cochon, porc
Collocations	
j?:n hmu: me: w: (TP)	**sense 1:** donnant donnant (Eq) tendre porc<n(m,s)> tendre chat<n(m,s)> (LT) l'un tend son cochon<n(m,s)> l'autre son chat<n(m,s)> (AS) contre une chose, une prestation équivalente à ce qu'on donne soi-même (FS) **sense 2:** donnant donnant (Eq) tendre porc<n(m,s)> tendre chat<n(m,s)> (LT) l'un tend son cochon<n(m,s)> l'autre son chat<n(m,s)> (AS) prendre son dû séance tenante dans une transaction (FS) **sense 3:** donnant donnant (Eq) tendre porc<n(m,s)> tendre chat<n(m,s)> (LT) l'un tend son cochon<n(m,s)> l'autre son chat<n(m,s)> (AS) vendre et acheter comptant (FS)

Figure 3. Polysemy illustrated by a Thai collocation with 3 functional senses (FS)

The linguistic phenomenon 'non reversibility of the lexis' is illustrated by the example shown in Figure 4.

French	English
Headword	
antécédents	'medical history'
Collocations	
antécédents du patient	patient history
antécédents médicaux	medical history

English	French
Headword	
history	–
Collocations	
patient history	antécédents du patient
medical history	antécédents médicaux

Figure 4. Illustration of non reversibility of the lexis

In this dictionary which is restricted to the domain of clinical research (Gavieiro 1998), even though there is a translation of the French headword *antécédents* by an English collocation '*medical history*' (printed between quotes to indicate it to be a collocation rather than a headword in the target language), this is not the case for the inverse sense for the English headword *history*. Being a dictionary of collocations, the translation of *history* as a headword has no place in such a domain specific dictionary. On the contrary, English collocations containing the headword *history* have their place, they are translated to French.

Lexicographic requirements can be divided into those which concern the functionality offered by the dictionary (for example, as we have already seen, the use of annotations for various purposes) and those which concern the organisation and integrity of the dictionary.

The functionality offered by such a dictionary includes the method of access to collocations as articles, the presentation of the articles in order to display any of the linguistic phenomena present (as has been illustrated by the examples above concerning synonymy, polysemy and non-reversibility of the lexis in translation), and the organisation and provision of lexicographical annotations.

For the access to collocations as articles this can be as in conventional paper dictionaries by means of headwords, typically in alphabetic order. A headword is an individual lexical unit whose primary purpose is to provide a means of access to a collocation. In the MultiCoDiCT system a headword is never the whole collocation even for a fully fixed expression. A given headword can access several collocations (as is illustrated in Figure 4) and in like manner, a collocation can be accessed by many headwords. This can be seen for the collocation *antécédents médicaux* with headwords *antécédents* (Figure 4) and *médical* (Figure 5).

French	English
Headword	
médical	medical
Collocations	
antécédents médicaux	medical history

Figure 5. Variant form of headword in the context of the collocation

The headwords of a collocation require to be specified; in the MultiCoDiCT system this is done explicitly by the lexicographer. Because of inflexional and derivational morphology, the headwords are typically in a canonical form, whilst the forms in the collocations can be variants; Figure 5 illustrates this for the French headword '*médical*' which takes the variant form '*médicaux*' in the French collocation. In Figure 4, the case of the headword *antécédents* (nominally a 'variant' (plural) of the canonical form *antécédent*) is atypical, the lexicographical choice of the form of the headword here being due to *antécédents* being a short form of *antécédents médicaux*. Thus in the organisation of the dictionary there must be, as is the case in the MultiCoDiCT system, a mapping between headwords in their canonical form and their 'presence' in collocations.

With annotations such as grammatical function (already shown in Figure 3) even the linguistic phenomenon of grammatical variation can be accounted for, as shown in Figure 6.

French	Spanish
Headword	
aérogare	terminal<n(m,s)> 'estación<n(f,s)> terminal <adj(f,s)>'

Figure 6. Illustration of grammatical variation

In the case of synonyms or polysemic equivalences, a given word can 'change' its grammatical role. In the first synonymic equivalence in the example in Figure 6, the Spanish word *terminal* is a noun whilst in the second it has as grammatical function adjective because the word *estación* has as role a noun. It should be noted that for the two grammatical functions of the word form *terminal*, in the Spanish lexis there is only one headword for *terminal*.

We now turn to the phenomena which have an impact on the organisation and integrity of such a dictionary and thus its underlying model and how this has been achieved in the MultiCoDiCT system. We must deal with variously collocations, headwords and annotations and the various interrelations between these such as sense groups and furthermore the relation between headwords and collocations, all these in a multilingual context. There must necessarily be some means to ensure the integrity of these various data items and the relations between them.

The model that underpins the MultiCoDiCT system is based on:

- firstly the sense group to which one or more collocations across one or more languages is associated in being sense equivalent (a sense group is no more than such an association),
- secondly the languages, to each of which collocations are uniquely associated,
- thirdly the collocations and
- fourthly the headwords, which in the MultiCoDiCT system are the only way to access directly a collocation and its sense equivalences (synonyms and translations). (Acces to collocations by means of linguistic phenomena is discussed in the next section.)

In respect of annotations, the underlying model allows these to be added at the level of sense group, collocation (for example regionalism) or collocation lexical item (for example grammatical category)

As far as the collocations which are the members of a sense group are concerned, these can be viewed orthogonally over two dimensions. One dimension involves the language and here too one or more languages may have a special status, such as Latin in dictionaries of flora and fauna which we address in the next section of the paper. The other dimension concerns the nature of collocations. Here we can type collocations as either being 'true' collocations in terms of the linguist's view, or, collocations which are translators' paraphrases such as for example translation types as we have already discussed and shown (Figure 3).

3 Linguistic phenomena and lexicographic attributes as a means of access

In this section we consider linguistic phenomena and by extension lexical attributes such as annotations of linguistic phenomena as themselves a means of access to the collocations in multilingual collocation dictionaries. We illustrate this approach by describing a bilingual dictionary of tourism that has been developed with this means of access in mind.

This dictionary involves the differences between French-Spanish-French translations found in ecological, fluvial and cultural (historical and religious) tourism corpora (Mendez, 1993; Rigole and Langlois, 2002). When translating the corpora, we noticed the presence of varieties of languages, such as Latin American Spanish and common Spanish (that is the Spanish of Spain) and of regionalisms; for example, in the case of Panama whose animal and plant specimen names were used only in that country and not in other Latin American countries, see Figure 7 (Chan 2005).

Common Spanish names	corozo	agutí
PANAMA	corozo	ñeque
BOLIVIA	totai	-
CUBA	-	jutía mocha
MEXICO	-	cotuza
VENEZUELA	corozo	zuliano de grupa negra
French translation	acrocome / coyol / noix de coyol	agouti

Figure 7. The presence of varieties of languages

We also found cases of linguistic phenomena at the semantic level, such as Americanisms, Anglicisms, non-reversible equivalents, etc. To handle these various observations we developed an algorithmic dictionary access method in order to provide access to the relevant collocations and translations. Our overall algorithm (see Figure 8) is itself composed of three principle sub-dictionaries:

a. French-Spanish-French equivalences (537 words),
b. particular cases at the semantic level (1146 words) and
c. particular cases at the grammatical level (291 sub-conditions).

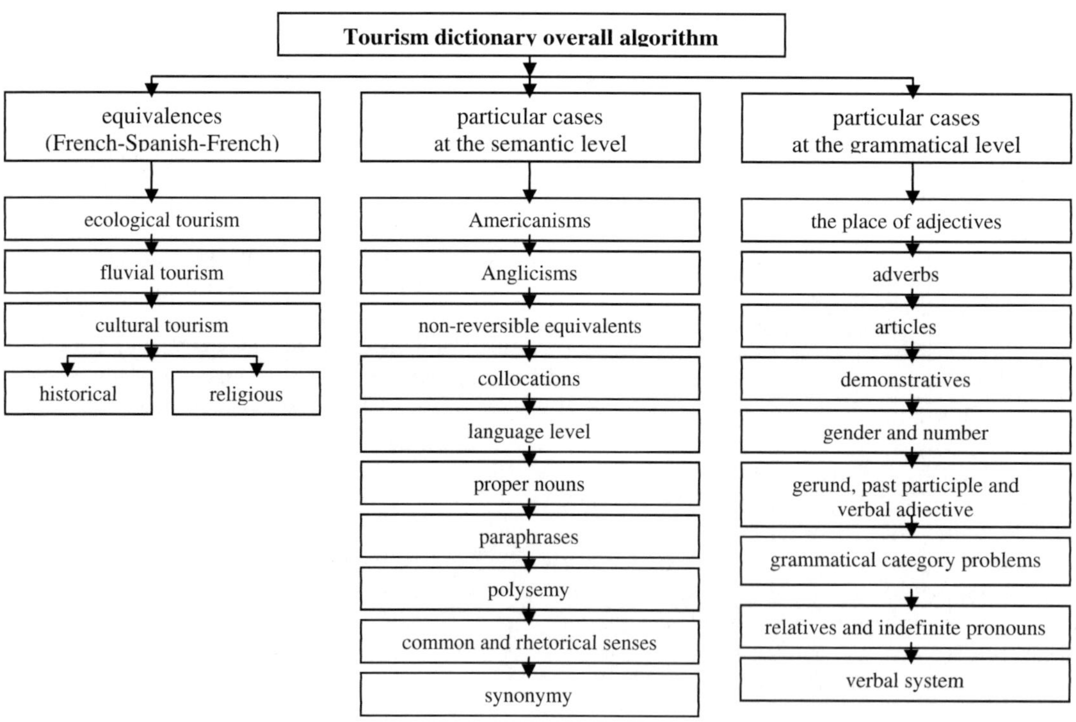

Figure 8. Dictionary access algorithm

The algorithm has a maximum of eight levels where the existence of other sub-dictionaries (or sub-algorithms) is possible inside of each dictionary, which itself can be consulted independently or dependently. In other words, the overall algorithm includes several mini-algorithms and mini-dictionaries.

At the start of each consultation, the words belonging to a given dictionary are presented in the form of a list arranged in alphabetical order so that the user can save time.

We now discuss these three specific sub-dictionaries.

The first sub-dictionary concerns equivalences which are provided in the French-Spanish-French languages and which are classified according to topic. The sub-field cultural tourism presents for example historical and religious tourism as sub-sub-fields.

The second sub-dictionary concerns particular cases at the semantic level, the terms of the dictionary of the Panamanian fauna, for example, are joined together by class such as: insects, mammals, birds and reptiles. The user can check starting from:

- French to obtain the equivalences in Spanish of Panama and common Spanish;
- French to obtain the equivalences in common Spanish and Latin;
- Panamanian Spanish to obtain the equivalences in common Spanish;
- common Spanish to obtain the equivalences in Panamanian Spanish;
- Panamanian Spanish and common Spanish to obtain the equivalences in French and Latin;
- Latin to obtain the equivalences in French, common Spanish and Panamanian Spanish.

At the outset we had the intention to develop a bilingual dictionary. However, we included Latin in the dictionary, since, when translating the Spanish corpora to French, we noticed that the names of the flora and fauna belonged to a specialised lexicon and that most of these names constituted regional variations. Thus, we had to look for the scientific name (coming from Latin), then the common Spanish name in bibliographical documents, monolingual dictionaries or on Internet sites dedicated to these fields and finally, to look for the French translation in general bilingual dictionaries (Spanish-French) and on zoological and botanical websites in order to validate the equivalences.

We did not consider the variants of other Latin-American countries because in order to do so it would have been necessary to undertake an intensive research exercise into the matter and to have had the terms checked by specialists in the field studied.

The third and last sub-dictionary deals with grammatical findings. It is not only composed of words but grammatical rules and also examples in order to illustrate the different cases. For this reason, we do not mention the quantity of words in the dictionary but rather the number of sub-conditions in the algorithm.

The algorithm that we have developed is interactively interpretable by the Studygram system (Cardey and Greenfield, 1992) which also provides the user interface. To illustrate the trace of a user access using our prototype system with the dictionary access algorithm illustrated in Figure 8, we take as entry the French collocation '*amazone à front rouge*' and where we are interested in the equivalences sub-dictionary and the particular cases sub-dictionary (see Figure 9).

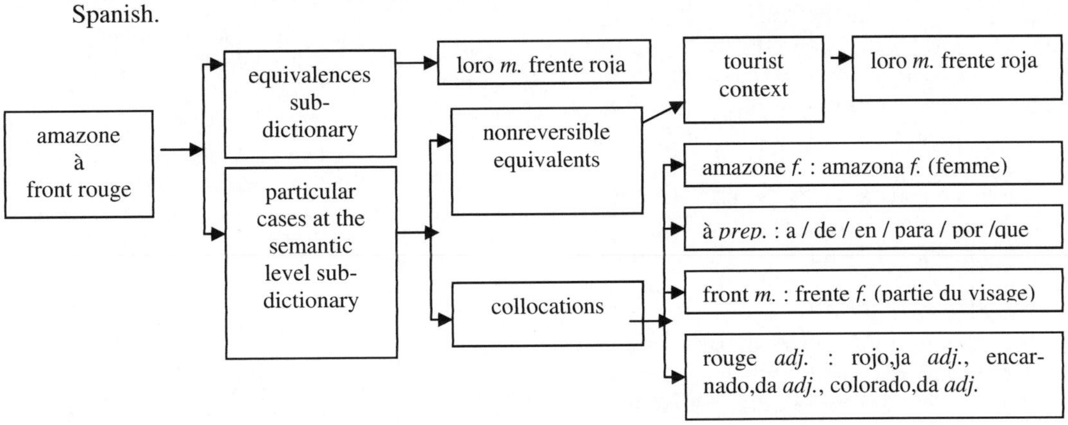

Figure 9. Trace of a user access with as entry the French collocation '*amazone à front rouge*'

4 Conclusion

We have presented the essential linguistic phenomena and the lexicographic requirements that we have discerned to be useful in the development of multilingual collocation dictionaries. By 'collocation' we mean not only set or fixed expressions including idioms, simple co-occurrences of items and metaphorical uses, but also translators' paraphrases. The basic model for such dictionaries as exemplified in the MultiCoDiCT system reposes on the concept of the collocation sense group as a means to ensure integrity and access. We have presented a novel access method to such dictionaries using the Studygram system which in essence provides access also based on much of the very linguistic phenomena and related lexicographical attributes that we have previously discerned and thus enabling access to collocations by posing a problem.

We conclude in showing how Studygram and MultiCoDiCT can be integrated in order to provide a more general approach for the access to such multilingual collocation dictionaries. In this approach, Studygram would provide the user interface and problem solving capability as described in section 3 and MultiCoDiCT would act as a lexical resources server.

At one level this approach would involve the essentially technical matter of standardising the mutual call mechanism (operational semantics) between Studygram and MultiCoDiCT. The Studygram system in any case supports algorithm solutions (called operations) which can be procedure calls, which in this context would be to MultiCoDiCT.

At another level this approach would involve formalising and standardising the linguistic and lexicographic terminology shared by the two systems. This level is thus concerned with including the lexicographical needs in the computational model. In respect of the semantics of the MultiCoDiCT component, the model underpinning MultiCoDiCT could be extended in a simple fashion to support explicitly the provision of linguistic 'headwords' involving the intrinsically modelled linguistic phenomena of synonymy and translation equivalences, polysemy and non-reversibility of the lexis. Access by conventional headwords is in any case already supported. The same MultiCoDiCT model provides annotation structures attached to the sense group, to the collocation and to the collocation lexical item. However the semantics of the annotation content is the lexicographer's and thus would involve an agreed semantics between the MuliCoDiCT and Stydygram components including the algorithm content concerning the machine interpretation of such annotation contents and lexicographic attributes.

References

Cardey, S., Greenfield P. 1992. The `Studygram' Natural Language Morphology System: A First Step to an Intelligent Tutoring Platform for Natural Language Morphology in *Proceedings of the UMIST ICALL workshop*, 42-59, published by CTI Centre for Modern Languages, University of Hull, UK

Cardey, S., Greenfield, P. 1999. Computerised set expression dictionaries : design and analysis, *Symposium on Contrastive Linguistics and Translation Studies* (Université Catholique de Louvain, Louvain-la-Neuve, Belgique) 5-6 February 1999. In Lexis in Contrast (B. Altenberg & S. Granger eds.), Benjamins.

Chan, R., 2005, El diccionario de la flora y fauna panameña: propuesta de algoritmo para la solución de problemas de traducción de español-francés, *IX Simposio Internacional de Comunicación Social, Santiago de Cuba*, 24-28 de enero 2005, Actas I, 389-393.

Gaveiro, E., 1998, Elaboration d'un Prototype de Dictionnaire Informatisé Français-Anglais / Anglais-Français. Application au Domaine de la Recherche Clinique, Mémoire de D.E.A., Université de Franche-Comté, France.

Greenfield, P. 1998a. L'espace de l'état et les invariants de l'état des dictionnaires terminologiques spécialisés de collocations multilingues, *Actes de la 1ère Rencontre Linguistique Méditerranéenne, Le Figement Lexical,* Tunis, les 17-18 et 19 September 1998, 271-283.

Greenfield, P. 1998b. Invariants in multilingual terminological dictionaries, *BULAG N° 3, ISBN 2-913322-11-5, Presses Universitaires Franc-Comtoises,* 1998, 111-121.

Greenfield, P. 2003. Le rôle de l'informatique dans le traitement et l'enseignement des langues, *Actes du Congrès international : Journées linguistiques franco-asiatiques,* Naresuan University, Phitsanulok, Thaïlande, 20-22 August 2003, 69-84.

Greenfield, P., Cardey, S., Achèche, S., Chan Ng, R., Galliot, J., Gavieiro, E., Morgadinho, H., Petit, E. 1999. Conception de systèmes de dictionnaires de collocations multilingues, le projet MultiCoDiCT, *Actes du Colloque international VIème Journées scientifiques du Réseau thématique de l'AUF Lexi-*

cologie, Terminologie, Traduction, Beyrouth, 11-13 November 1999, 103-113.

Mendez, E. 1993. *Los roedores de Panamá.* Panamá, Laboratorio Conmemorativo Gorgas, pp.59-64 and pp.281-286.

Moon, R. 1998. *Fixed expressions and idioms in English, a corpus-based approach.* Clarendon Press, Oxford. ISBN 0-19823614-X.

Rigole, M., Langlois, C-V. 2002. *Panamá. Guides de voyage ULYSSE.* 4th edition. Canada, Guides de voyage Ulysse inc., 333p.

Spivey, J.M. 1992. *The Z Notation.* Prentice Hall, ISBN 0-13-978529-9.

Werthe-Hengsanga, V. 2001. *Etude de la traduction automatique en français des expressions imagées de la langue thaï (domaine animalier).* DEA, Sciences du langage, Université de Franche-Comté, Besançon, France.

Multilingual Collocation Extraction: Issues and Solutions

Violeta Seretan
Language Technology Laboratory
University of Geneva
2, rue de Candolle, 1211 Geneva
Violeta.Seretan@latl.unige.ch

Eric Wehrli
Language Technology Laboratory
University of Geneva
2, rue de Candolle, 1211 Geneva
Eric.Wehrli@latl.unige.ch

Abstract

Although traditionally seen as a language-independent task, collocation extraction relies nowadays more and more on the linguistic preprocessing of texts (e.g., lemmatization, POS tagging, chunking or parsing) prior to the application of statistical measures. This paper provides a language-oriented review of the existing extraction work. It points out several language-specific issues related to extraction and proposes a strategy for coping with them. It then describes a hybrid extraction system based on a multilingual parser. Finally, it presents a case-study on the performance of an association measure across a number of languages.

1 Introduction

Collocations are understood in this paper as "idiosyncratic syntagmatic combination of lexical items" (Fontenelle, 1992, 222): *heavy rain*, *light breeze*, *great difficulty*, *grow steadily*, *meet requirement*, *reach consensus*, *pay attention*, *ask a question*. Unlike idioms (*kick the bucket*, *lend a hand*, *pull someone's leg*), their meaning is fairly transparent and easy to decode. Yet, differently from the regular productions, (*big house*, *cultural activity*, *read a book*), collocational expressions are highly idiosyncratic, since the lexical items a headword combines with in order to express a given meaning is contingent upon that word (Mel'čuk, 2003).

This is apparent when comparing a collocation's equivalents across different languages. The English collocation *ask a question* translates as *poser une question* in French (lit., ?*put a question*), and as *fare una domanda*, *hacer una pregunta* in Italian and Spanish (lit., *to make a question*).

As it has been pointed out by many researchers (Cruse, 1986; Benson, 1990; McKeown and Radev, 2000), collocations cannot be described by means of general syntactic and semantic rules. They are arbitrary and unpredictable, and therefore need to be memorized and used as such. They constitute the so-called "semi-finished products" of language (Hausmann, 1985) or the "islands of reliability" (Lewis, 2000) on which the speakers build their utterances.

2 Motivation

The key importance of collocations in text production tasks such as machine translation and natural language generation has been stressed many times. It has been equally shown that collocations are useful in a range of other applications, such as word sense disambiguation (Brown et al., 1991) and parsing (Alshawi and Carter, 1994).

The NLP community fully acknowledged the need for an appropriate treatment of multi-word expressions in general (Sag et al., 2002). Collocations are particularly important because of their prevalence in language, regardless of the domain or genre. According to Jackendoff (1997, 156) and Mel'čuk (1998, 24), collocations constitute the bulk of a language's lexicon.

The last decades have witnessed a considerable development of collocation extraction techniques, that concern both monolingual and (parallel) multilingual corpora.

We can mention here only part of this work: (Berry-Rogghe, 1973; Church et al., 1989; Smadja, 1993; Lin, 1998; Krenn and Evert, 2001) for monolingual extraction, and (Kupiec, 1993; Wu, 1994; Smadja et al., 1996; Kitamura and Mat-

Proceedings of the Workshop on Multilingual Language Resources and Interoperability, pages 40–49,
Sydney, July 2006. ©2006 Association for Computational Linguistics

sumoto, 1996; Melamed, 1997) for bilingual extraction via alignment.

Traditionally, collocation extraction was considered a language-independent task. Since collocations are recurrent, typical lexical combinations, a wide range of statistical methods based on word co-occurrence frequency have been heavily used for detecting them in text corpora. Among the most often used types of lexical association measures (henceforth AMs) we mention: *statistical hypothesis tests* (e.g., binomial, Poisson, Fisher, z-score, chi-squared, t-score, and log-likelihood ratio tests), that measure the significance of the association between two words based on a contingency table listing their joint and marginal frequency, and *Information-theoretic measures* (Mutual Information — henceforth MI — and its variants), that quantity of 'information' shared by two random variables. A detailed review of the statistical methods employed in collocation extraction can be found, for instance, in (Evert, 2004). A comprehensive list of AMs is given (Pecina, 2005).

Very often, in addition to the information on co-occurrence frequency, language-specific information is also integrated in a collocation extraction system (as it will be seen in section 3):

- morphological information, in order to count inflected word forms as instances of the same base form. For instance, *ask questions*, *asks question*, *asked question* are all instances of the same word pair, *ask - question*;

- syntactic information, in order to recognize a word pair even if subject to (complex) syntactic transformations: *ask multiple questions*, *question asked*, *questions that one might ask*.

The language-specific modules thus aim at coping with the problem of morphosyntactic variation, in order to improve the accuracy of frequency information. This becomes truly important especially for free-word order and for high-inflection languages, for which the token(form)-based frequency figures become too skewed due to the high lexical dispersion. Not only the data scattering modify the frequency numbers used by AMs, but it also alters the performance of AMs, if the the probabilities in the contingency table become very low.

Morphosyntactic information has in fact been shown to significantly improve the extraction results (Breidt, 1993; Smadja, 1993; Zajac et al., 2003). Morphological tools such as lemmatizers and POS taggers are being commonly used in extraction systems; they are employed both for dealing with text variation and for validating the candidate pairs: combinations of function words are typically ruled out (Justeson and Katz, 1995), as are the ungrammatical combinations in the systems that make use of parsers (Church and Hanks, 1990; Smadja, 1993; Basili et al., 1994; Lin, 1998; Goldman et al., 2001; Seretan et al., 2004).

Given the motivations for performing a linguistically-informed extraction — which were also put forth, among others, by Church and Hanks (1990, 25), Smadja (1993, 151) and Heid (1994) — and given the recent development of linguistic analysis tools, it seems plausible that the linguistic structure will be more and more taken into account by collocation extraction systems.

The rest of the paper is organized as follows. In section 3 we provide a language-oriented review of the existing collocation extraction work. Then we highlight, in section 4, a series of problems that arise in the transfer of methodology to a new language, and we propose a strategy for dealing with them. Section 5 describes an extraction system, and, finally, section 6 presents a case-study on the collocations extracted for four languages, illustrating the cross-lingual variation in the performance of a particular AM.

3 Overview of Extraction Work

3.1 English

As one might expect, the bulk of the collocation extraction work concerns the English language: (Choueka, 1988; Church et al., 1989; Church and Hanks, 1990; Smadja, 1993; Justeson and Katz, 1995; Kjellmer, 1994; Sinclair, 1995; Lin, 1998), among many others[1].

Choueka's method (1988) detects *n*-grams (adjacent words) only, by simply computing the co-occurrence frequency. Justeson and Katz (1995) apply a POS-filter on the pairs they extract. As in (Kjellmer, 1994), the AM they use is the simple frequency.

Smadja (1993) employs the z-score in conjunction with several heuristics (e.g., the systematic occurrence of two lexical items at the same distance in text) and extracts predicative collocations,

[1]E.g., (Frantzi et al., 2000; Pearce, 2001; Goldman et al., 2001; Zaiu Inkpen and Hirst, 2002; Dias, 2003; Seretan et al., 2004; Pecina, 2005), and the list can be continued.

rigid noun phrases and phrasal templates. He then uses the a parser in order to validate the results. The parsing is shown to lead to an increase in accuracy from 40% to 80%.

(Church et al., 1989) and (Church and Hanks, 1990) use POS information and a parser to extract verb-object pairs, which then they rank according to the mutual information (MI) measure they introduce.

Lin's (1998) is also a hybrid approach that relies on a dependency parser. The candidates extracted are then ranked with MI.

3.2 German

German is the second most investigated language, thanks to the early work of Breidt (1993) and, more recently, to that of Krenn and Evert, such as (Krenn and Evert, 2001; Evert and Krenn, 2001; Evert, 2004) centered on evaluation.

Breidt uses MI and t-score and compares the results accuracy when various parameters vary, such as the window size, presence vs. absence of lemmatization, corpus size, and presence vs. absence of POS and syntactic information. She focuses on N-V pairs[2] and, despite the lack of syntactic analysis tools at the time, by simulating parsing she comes to the conclusion that "Very high precision rates, which are an indispensable requirement for lexical acquisition, can only realistically be envisaged for German with parsed corpora" (Breidt, 1993, 82).

Later, Krenn and Evert (2001) used a German chunker to extract syntactic pairs such as P-N-V. Their work put the basis of formal and systematic methods in collocation extraction evaluation. Zinsmeister and Heid (2003; 2004) focused on N-V and A-N-V combinations identified using a stochastic parser. They applied machine learning techniques in combination to the log-likelihood measure (henceforth LL) for distinguishing trivial compounds from lexicalized ones.

Finally, Wermter and Hahn (2004) identified PP-V combinations using a POS tagger and a chunker. They based their method on a linguistic criterion (that of limited modifiability) and compared their results with those obtained using the t-score and LL tests.

[2]The following abbreviations are used in this paper: N - noun, V - verb, A - adjective, Adv - adverb, Det - determiner, Conj - conjunction, P - preposition.

3.3 French

Thanks to the outstanding work of Gross on lexicon-grammar (1984), French is one of the most studied languages in terms of distributional and transformational potential of words. This work has been carried out before the computer era and the advent of corpus linguistics, while automatic extraction was later performed, for instance, in (Lafon, 1984; Daille, 1994; Bourigault, 1992; Goldman et al., 2001).

Daille (1994) aimed at extracting compound nouns, defined a priori by means of certain syntactic patterns, like N-A, N-N, N-à-N, N-de-N, N P Det N. She used a lemmatizer and a POS-tagger before applying a series of AMs, which she then evaluated against a domain-specific terminology dictionary and against a gold-standard manually created from the extraction corpus.

Similarly, Bourigault (1992) extracted noun-phrases from shallow-parsed text, and Goldman et al. (2001) extracted syntactic collocations by using a full parser and applying the LL test.

3.4 Other Languages

In addition to English, German and French, other languages for which notable collocation extraction work was performed, are — as we are aware of — the following:

- Italian: early extraction work was carried out by Calzolari and Bindi (1990) and employed MI. It was followed by (Basili et al., 1994), that made use of parsing information;
- Korean: (Shimohata et al., 1997) used an adjacency *n*-gram model, and (Kim et al., 1999) relied on POS-tagging;
- Chinese: (Huang et al., 2005) used POS information, while (Lu et al., 2004) applied extraction techniques similar to Xtract system (Smadja, 1993);
- Japanese: (Ikehara et al., 1995) was based on an improved *n*-gram method.

As for multilingual extraction via alignment (where collocations are first detected in one language and then matched with their translation in another language), most or the existing work concern the English-French language pair, and the Hansard corpus of Canadian Parliament proceedings. Wu (1994) signals a number of problems that non-Indo-European languages pose for the existing alignment methods based on word- and sentence-length: in Chinese, for instance, most of the words are just one or two characters long, and there are no word delimiters. This result suggests that the portability of existing alignment methods to new language pairs is questionable.

We are not concerned here with extraction via alignment. We assume, instead, that multilingual support in collocation extraction means the customization of the extraction procedure for each language. This topic will be addressed in the next sections.

4 Multilingualism: Why and How?

4.1 Some Issues

As the previous section showed, many systems of collocation extraction rely on the linguistic preprocessing of source corpora in order to support the candidate identification process. Language-specific information, such as the one derived from morphological and syntactic analysis, was shown to be highly beneficial for extraction. Moreover, the possibility to apply the association measures on syntactically homogenous material is argued to benefit extraction, as the performance of association measures might vary with the syntactic configurations because of the differences in distribution (Krenn and Evert, 2001).

The lexical distribution is therefore a relevant issue from the perspective of multilingual collocation extraction. Different languages show different proportions of lexical categories (N, V, A, Adv, P, etc.) which are evenly distributed across syntactic types[3]. Depending on the frequency numbers, a given AM could be more suited for a specific syntactic configuration in one language, and less suited for the same configuration in another. Ideally, each language should be assigned a suitable set of AMs to be applied on syntactically-homogenous data.

Another issue that is relevant in the multilingualism perspective is that of the syntactic configurations characterizing collocations. Several such relations (e.g., noun-adjectival modifier, predicate-argument) are likely to remain constant through languages, i.e., to be judged as collocationally interesting in many languages. However, other configurations could be language-specific (like P-N-V in German, whose English equivalent is V-P-N). Yet other configurations might have no counterpart at all in another language (e.g., the French P-A pair *à neuf* is translated into English as a Conj-A pair, *as new*).

Finding all the collocationally-relevant syntactic types for a language is therefore another problem that has to be solved in multilingual extraction. Since a priori defining these types based on intuition does not ensure the necessary coverage, an alternative proposal is to induce them from POS data and dependency relations, as in (Seretan, 2005).

The morphoyntactic differences between languages also have to be taken into account. With English as the most investigated language, several hypotheses were put forth in extraction and became common place.

For instance, using a 5-words window as search space for collocation pairs is a usual practice, since this span length was shown sufficient to cover a high percentage of syntactic co-occurrences in English. But — as suggested by other researchers, e.g., (Goldman et al., 2001) —, this assumption does not necessary hold for other languages.

Similarly, the higher inflection and the higher transformation potential shown by some languages pose additional problems in extraction, which were rather ignored for English. As Kim et al. (1999) notice, collocation extraction is particularly difficult in free-order languages like Korean, where arguments scramble freely. Breidt (1993) also pointed out a couple of problems that makes extraction for German more difficult than for English: the strong inflection for verbs, the variable word-order, and the positional ambiguity of the arguments. She shows that even distinguishing subjects from objects is very difficult without parsing.

4.2 A Strategy for Multilingual Extraction

Summing up the previous discussion, the customization of collocation extraction for a given language needs to take into account:

- the syntactic configurations characterizing collocations,
- the lexical distribution over syntactic configurations,
- the adequacy of AMs to these configurations.

[3] For instance, V-P pairs are more represented in English than in other languages (as phrasal verbs or verb-particle constructions).

These are language-specific parameters which need to be set in a successful multilingual extraction procedure. Truly multilingual systems have not been developed yet, but we suggest the following strategy for building such a system:

A. parse the source corpus, extract all the syntactic pairs (e.g., head-modifier, predicate-argument) and rank them with a given AM,

B. analyze the results and find the syntactic configurations characterizing collocations,

C. evaluate the adequacy of AMs for ranking collocations in each syntactic configuration, and find the most convenient mapping configurations - AMs.

Once customized for a language, the extraction procedure involves:

Stage 1. parsing the source corpus for extracting the lexical pairs in the relevant, language-specific syntactic configurations found in step B;

Stage 2. ranking the pairs from each syntactic class with the AM assigned in step C.

5 A Multilingual Collocation Extractor Based on Parsing

Ever since the collocation was brought to the attention of linguists in the framework of contextualism (Firth, 1957; Firth, 1968), it has been preponderantly seen as a pure statistical phenomenon of lexical association. In fact, according to a well-known definition, "a collocation is an arbitrary and recurrent word combination" (Benson, 1990).

This approach was at the basis of the computational work on collocation, although there exist an alternative approach — the linguistic, or lexicographic one — that imposes a restricted view on collocation, which is seen first of all as an expression of language.

The existing extraction work (section 3) shows that there is a growing interest in adopting the more restricted (linguistic) view. As mentioned in section 3, the importance of parsing for extraction was confirmed by several evaluation experiments. With the recent development in the field of linguistic analysis, hybrid extraction systems (i.e., systems relying on syntactical analysis for collocation extraction) are likely to become the rule rather than the exception.

Our system (Goldman et al., 2001; Seretan and Wehrli, 2006) is — to our knowledge — the first to perform the full syntactic analysis as support for collocation extraction; similar approaches rely on dependency parsers or on chunking.

It is based on a symbolic parser that was developed over the last decade (Wehrli, 2004) and achieves a high level of performance, in terms of accuracy, speed and robustness. The languages it supports are, for the time being, French, English, Italian, Spanish and German. A few other languages are being also implemented in the framework of a multilingualism project.

Provided that collocation extraction can be seen as a two-stage process (where, in stage 1, collocation candidates are identified in the text corpora, and in stage 2, they are ranked according to a given AM, cf. section 4.2), the role of the parser is to support the first stage. A pair of lexical items is selected as a candidate only if there exist a syntactic relation holding between the two items.

Unlike the traditional, window-based methods, candidate selection is based on syntactic proximity (as opposed to textual proximity). Another peculiarity of our system is that candidate pairs are identified as the parsing goes on; in other approaches, they are extracted by post-processing the output of syntactic tools.

The candidate pairs identified are classified into syntactically homogenous sets, according to the syntactic relations holding between the two items. Only certain predefined syntactic relations are kept, that were judged as collocationally relevant after multiple experiments of extraction and data analysis (e.g., adjective-noun, verb-object, subject-verb, noun-noun, verb-preposition-noun). The sets obtained are then ranked using the log-likelihood ratios test (Dunning, 1993).

More details about the system and its performance can be found in (Seretan and Wehrli, 2006). The following examples (taken from the extraction experiment we will describe below) illustrate its potential to detect collocation candidates, even if these are subject to complex syntactic transformations:

1.a) *atteindre objectif* (Fr): Les *objectifs* fixés à l'échelle internationale visant à réduire les émissions ne peuvent pas être *atteints* à l'aide de ces seuls programmes.

1.b) *accogliere emendamento* (It):

Posso pertanto *accogliere* in parte e in linea di principio gli *emendamenti* nn. 43-46 e l'emendamento n. 85.

1.c) *reforzar cooperación* (Es): Queremos permitir a los pases que lo deseen *reforzar*, en un contexto unitario, su *cooperación* en cierto número de sectores.

The collocation extractor is part of a bigger system (Seretan et al., 2004) that integrates a concordancer and a sentence aligner, and that supports the visualization, the manual validation and the management of a multilingual terminology database. The validated collocations are used for populating the lexicon of the parser and that of a translation system (Wehrli, 2003).

6 A Cross-Lingual Extraction Experiment

A collocation extraction experiment concerning four different languages (English, Spanish, French, Italian) has been conducted on a parallel subcorpus of 42 files from the European Parliament proceedings. Several statistics and extraction results are reported in Table 1.

Statistics	English	Spanish	Italian	French
tokens	2526403	2666764	2575858	2938118
sent/file	2329.1	2513.7	2331.6	2392.8
complete parses	63.4%	35.5%	46.8%	63.7%
tokens/sent	25.8	25.3	26.3	29.2
extr. pairs (tokens)	617353	568998	666122	565287
token/type	2.6	2.5	2.3	2.3
LL is def.	85.9%	90.6%	83.5%	92.8%

Table 1: Extraction statistics

We computed the distribution of pair tokens according to the syntactic type and noted that the most marked distributional difference among these languages concern the following types: N-A (7.12), A-N (4.26), V-O (2.68), V-P (4.16), N-P-N (3.81)[4].

Unsurprisingly, the Romance languages are less different in terms of syntactic co-occurrence distribution, and the deviation of English from the Romance mean is more pronounced — in particular, for N-A (9.72), V-P (5.63), A-N (5.25), N-P-N (4.77), and V-O (3.57). These distributional differences might account for the types of collocations highlighted by a particular AM (such as LL) in a language vs. another. Figure 1 displays the relative proportions of 3 syntactic types — adjective-noun, subject-verb and verb-object — that can be found at different levels in the significance list returned by LL.

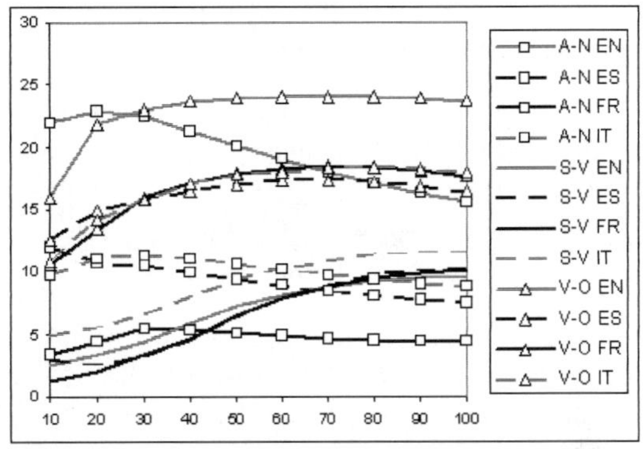

Figure 1: Cross-lingual proportions of A-N, S-V and V-O pairs at different levels in the significance lists

We performed a contrastive analysis of results, by carrying out a case-study aimed at checking the LL performance variability across languages. The study concerned the verb-object collocations having the noun *policy* as the direct object. We specifically focused on the best-scored collocation extracted from the French corpus, namely *mener une politique* (lit., *conduct a policy*).

We looked at the translation equivalents of its 74 instances identified by our extraction system in the corpus. The analysis revealed that — at least in this particular case — the verbal collocates of this noun are highly scattered: *pursue, implement, conduct, adopt, apply, develop, have, draft, launch, run, carry out* for English; *practicar, llevar a cabo, desarrollar, realizar, aplicar, seguir, hacer, adoptar, ejercer* for Spanish; *condurre, attuare, portare avanti, perseguire, praticare, adottare, fare* for Italian (among several others). Some of the collocates (those listed first) are more prominently used. But generally they are highly dispersed, and this might indicate a bigger difficulty for LL to pinpoint the best collocate in a language vs. another.

We also observed that quite frequently (in about 25% of the cases) the collocation did not conserve its syntactic configuration. Either the verb — here,

[4]The numbers represent the values the standard deviation of the relative percentages in the whole lists of pairs.

the equivalent for the French *mener* — is omitted in translations (like in 2.b below):

2.a) des contradictions existent dans la politique qui est menée (Fr);

2.b) we are dealing with contradictory policy (En),

or, in a few other cases, the whole collocation disappears, since paraphrased with a completely different syntactic construction:

3.a) direction qui a mené une politique insensée de réduction de personnel (Fr);

3.b) a management that foolishly engaged in staff reductions (En).

In order to quantify the impact such factors have on the performance of the AM considered, we further scrutinized the collocates list for *politique* proposed by LL test for each language (see Table 2). The rank of a pair in the whole list of verb-object collocations extracted, as assigned by the LL test, is shown in the last column. In these significance lists, the collocations with *politique* as an object constitute a small fraction, and from these, only the top collocations are displayed in Table 2. The threshold was manually defined in accordance with our intuition that the lower-scored pairs observed manifest less a collocational strength. It happens to be situated around the LL value of 20 for each language (and is of course specific to the size of our corpus and to the number of V-O tokens identified therein).

If we consider the LL rank as the success measure for collocate detection, we can infer that the collocates of the word under investigation are easier to found in French, as compared to English, Italian or Spanish, because the value in the first row of the last column is smaller. This holds if we are interested in only one (the most salient) collocate for a word.

If we measure the success of retrieving all the collocates (by considering, for instance, the speed to access them in the results list — the higher the rank, the better), then French can be again considered the easiest because overall, the positions in the V-O list are higher (i.e., the mean of the rank column is smaller) with respect to Spanish, Italian and, respectively, English.

This latter result corresponds, approximately, to the order given by relative proportion of V-O

Language	**collocate**	**freq**	**LL score**	**rank**
French	mener	74	376.8	45
politique	élaborer	17	50.1	734
	adapter	5	48.3	780
	axer	8	41.4	955
	pratiquer	9	39.7	1011
	développer	13	28.1	1599
	adapter	8	25.2	1867
	poursuivre	11	24.4	1943
English	pursue	39	214.9	122
policy	implement	38	108.7	325
	develop	30	81.1	473
	conduct	8	28.9	2014
	harmonize	9	28.2	2090
	gear	5	27.7	2201
	need	25	24.9	2615
	apply	16	23.3	2930
Spanish	practicar	17	98.7	246
política	desarrollar	27	82.4	312
	aplicar	25	65.7	431
	seguir	17	33.5	1003
	coordinar	8	31.0	1112
	basar	11	25.1	1473
	orientar	6	22.5	1707
	adaptar	5	20.0	1987
	construir	6	19.4	2057
Italian	attuare	23	79.5	382
politica	perseguire	14	46.4	735
	praticare	8	37.6	976
	seguire	18	30.2	1314
	portare	12	29.7	1348
	rivedere	9	26.0	1607
	riformare	7	25.6	1639
	sviluppare	12	22.1	1975
	adottare	20	21.2	2087

Table 2: Verbal collocates for the headword *policy*

pairs in each language (Spanish 15.12%, French 15.14%, Italian 17.06%, and English 20.82%). Given that in English V-O pairs are more numerous and the verbs also participate in V-P constructions, it might seem reasonable to expect lower LL scores for V-O collocations in English vs. the other 3 languages.

In general, we expect a correlation between extraction difficulty and the distributional properties of co-occurrence types.

7 Conclusion

The paper pointed out several issues that occur in transfering a hybrid collocation extraction methodology (that combines linguistic with statistic information) to a new language.

Besides the questionable availability of language-specific text analysis tools for the new language, a number of issues that are relevant to extraction proper were addressed: the changes in the distribution of (syntactic) word pairs, and the need to find, for each language, the most appropriate association measure to apply for each syntactic type (given that AMs are sensitive to distributions and syntactic types); the lack of a priori defined syntactic types for a language; and, finally, the portability of some widely used techniques (such as the window method) from English to other languages exhibiting a higher word order freedom.

It is again in the multilingualism perspective that the inescapable need for preprocessing the text emerged (cf. different researchers cited in section 3): highly inflected languages need lemmatizers, free-word order languages need structural information in order to guarantee acceptable results. As language tools become nowadays more and more available, we expect the collocation extraction (and terminology acquisition in general) to be exclusively performed in the future by relying on linguistic analysis. We therefore believe that multilingualism is a true concern for collocation extraction.

The paper reviewed the extraction work in a language-oriented fashion, while mentioning the type of linguistic preprocessing performed whenever it was the case, as well as the language-specific issues identified by the authors. It then proposed a strategy for implementing a multilingual extraction procedure that takes into account the language-specific issues identified.

An extraction system for four different languages, based on full parsing, was then described. Finally, an experiment was carried out as a case study, which pointed out several factors that might determine a particular AM to perform differently across languages. The experiment suggested that log-likelihood ratios test might highlight certain verb-object collocations easier in French than in Spanish, Italian and English (in terms of salience in the significance list).

Future work needs to extend the type of cross-linguistic analysis initiated here, in order to provide more insights on the differences expected at extraction between one language and another and on the responsible factors, and, accordingly, to defines strategies to deal with them.

Acknowledgements

The research described in this paper has been supported in part by a grant from the Swiss National Foundation (No. 101412-103999).

References

Hiyan Alshawi and David Carter. 1994. Training and scaling preference functions for disambiguation. *Computational Linguistics*, 20(4):635–648.

Roberto Basili, Maria Teresa Pazienza, and Paola Velardi. 1994. A "not-so-shallow" parser for collocational analysis. In *Proceedings of the 15th conference on Computational linguistics*, pages 447–453, Kyoto, Japan. Association for Computational Linguistics.

Morton Benson. 1990. Collocations and general-purpose dictionaries. *International Journal of Lexicography*, 3(1):23–35.

Godelieve L. M. Berry-Rogghe. 1973. The computation of collocations and their relevance to lexical studies. In A. J. Aitken, R. W. Bailey, and N. Hamilton-Smith, editors, *The Computer and Literary Studies*, pages 103–112. Edinburgh.

Didier Bourigault. 1992. Surface grammatical analysis for the extraction of terminological noun phrases. In *Proceedings of the 15th International Conference on Computational Linguistics*, pages 977–981, Nantes, France.

Elisabeth Breidt. 1993. Extraction of V-N-collocations from text corpora: A feasibility study for German. In *Proceedings of the Workshop on Very Large Corpora: Academic and Industrial Perspectives*, Columbus, U.S.A.

Peter F. Brown, Stephen A. Della Pietra, Vincent J. Della Pietra, and Robert L. Mercer. 1991. Word-sense disambiguation using statistical methods. In *Proceedings of the 29th Annual Meeting of the Association for Computational Linguistics (ACL 1991)*, pages 264–270, Berkeley, California.

Nicoletta Calzolari and Remo Bindi. 1990. Acquisition of lexical information from a large textual Italian corpus. In *Proceedings of the 13th International Conference on Computational Linguistics*, pages 54–59, Helsinki, Finland.

Yaacov Choueka. 1988. Looking for needles in a haystack, or locating interesting collocational expressions in large textual databases. In *Proceedings of the International Conference on User-Oriented Content-Based Text and Image Handling*, pages 609–623, Cambridge, U.S.A.

Kenneth Church and Patrick Hanks. 1990. Word association norms, mutual information, and lexicography. *Computational Linguistics*, 16(1):22–29.

Kenneth Church, William Gale, Patrick Hanks, and Donald Hindle. 1989. Parsing, word associations and typical predicate-argument relations. In *Proceedings of the International Workshop on Parsing Technologies*, pages 103–112, Pittsburgh. Carnegie Mellon University.

D. Alan Cruse. 1986. *Lexical Semantics*. Cambridge University Press, Cambridge.

Béatrice Daille. 1994. *Approche mixte pour l'extraction automatique de terminologie : statistiques lexicales et filtres linguistiques*. Ph.D. thesis, Université Paris 7.

Gaël Dias. 2003. Multiword unit hybrid extraction. In *Proceedings of the ACL Workshop on Multiword Expressions*, pages 41–48, Sapporo, Japan.

Ted Dunning. 1993. Accurate methods for the statistics of surprise and coincidence. *Computational Linguistics*, 19(1):61–74.

Stefan Evert and Brigitte Krenn. 2001. Methods for the qualitative evaluation of lexical association measures. In *Proceedings of the 39th Annual Meeting of the Association for Computational Linguistics*, pages 188–195, Toulouse, France.

Stefan Evert. 2004. *The Statistics of Word Cooccurrences: Word Pairs and Collocations*. Ph.D. thesis, University of Stuttgart.

John Rupert Firth, 1957. *Papers in Linguistics 1934-1951*, chapter Modes of Meaning, pages 190–215. Oxford Univ. Press, Oxford.

J. R. Firth. 1968. A synopsis of linguistic theory, 1930–55. In F.R. Palmer, editor, *Selected papers of J. R. Firth, 1952-1959*. Indiana University Press, Bloomington.

Thierry Fontenelle. 1992. Collocation acquisition from a corpus or from a dictionary: a comparison. *Proceedings I-II. Papers submitted to the 5th EURALEX International Congress on Lexicography in Tampere*, pages 221–228.

Katerina T. Frantzi, Sophia Ananiadou, and Hideki Mima. 2000. Automatic recognition of multi-word terms: the C-value/NC-value method. *International Journal on Digital Libraries*, 2(3):115–130.

Jean-Philippe Goldman, Luka Nerima, and Eric Wehrli. 2001. Collocation extraction using a syntactic parser. In *Proceedings of the ACL Workshop on Collocations*, pages 61–66, Toulouse, France.

Maurice Gross. 1984. Lexicon-grammar and the syntactic analysis of French. In *Proceedings of the 22nd conference on Association for Computational Linguistics*, pages 275–282, Morristown, NJ, USA.

Franz Iosef Hausmann. 1985. Kollokationen im deutschen wörterbuch. ein beitrag zur theorie des lexikographischen beispiels". In Henning Bergenholtz and Joachim Mugdan, editors, *Lezikographie und Grammatik. Akten des Essener Kolloquiums zur Grammatik im Wörterbuch.*, Lexicographica. Series Major 3, pages 118–129.

Ulrich Heid. 1994. On ways words work together - research topics in lexical combinatorics. In W. Martin, W. Meijs, M. Moerland, E. ten Pas, P. van Sterkenburg, and P. Vossen, editors, *Proceedings of the VIth Euralex International Congress (EURALEX '94)*, pages 226–257, Amsterdam.

Chu-Ren Huang, Adam Kilgarriff, Yiching Wu, Chih-Ming Chiu, Simon Smith, Pavel Rychly, Ming-Hong Bai, and Keh-Jiann Chen. 2005. Chinese Sketch Engine and the extraction of grammatical collocations. In *Proceedings of the Fourth SIGHAN Workshop on Chinese Language Processing*, pages 48–55, Jeju Island, Republic of Korea.

Satoru Ikehara, Satoshi Shirai, and Tsukasa Kawaoka. 1995. Automatic extraction of uninterrupted collocations by n-gram statistics. In *Proceedings of first Annual Meeting of the Association for Natural Language Processing*, pages 313–316.

Ray Jackendoff. 1997. *The Architecture of the Language Faculty*. MIT Press, Cambridge, MA.

John S. Justeson and Slava M. Katz. 1995. Technical terminology: Some linguistis properties and an algorithm for identification in text. *Natural Language Engineering*, 1:9–27.

Seonho Kim, Zooil Yang, Mansuk Song, and Jung-Ho Ahn. 1999. Retrieving collocations from Korean text. In *Proceedings of the 1999 Joint SIGDAT Conference on Empirical Methods in Natural Language Processing and Very Large Corpora*, pages 71–81, Maryland, U.S.A.

Mihoko Kitamura and Yuji Matsumoto. 1996. Automatic extraction of word sequence correspondences in parallel corpora. In *Proceedings of the 4th Workshop on Very Large Corpora*, pages 79–87, Copenhagen, Denmark, August.

Göran Kjellmer. 1994. *A Dictionary of English Collocations*. Claredon Press, Oxford.

Brigitte Krenn and Stefan Evert. 2001. Can we do better than frequency? A case study on extracting PP-verb collocations. In *Proceedings of the ACL Workshop on Collocations*, pages 39–46, Toulouse, France.

Julian Kupiec. 1993. An algorithm for finding noun phrase correspondences in bilingual corpora. In *31st Annual Meeting of the Association for Computational Linguistics*, pages 17–22, Columbus, Ohio, U.S.A.

P. Lafon. 1984. *Dépouillement et statistique en léxicometrie*. Slatkine-Champion, Paris.

Michael Lewis. 2000. *Teaching Collocations. Further Developments In The Lexical Approach*. Language Teaching Publications, Hove.

Dekang Lin. 1998. Extracting collocations from text corpora. In *First Workshop on Computational Terminology*, pages 57–63, Montreal.

Qin Lu, Yin Li, and Ruifeng Xu. 2004. Improving Xtract for Chinese collocation extraction. In *Proceedings of IEEE International Conference on Natural Language Processing and Knowledge Engineering*, pages 333–338.

Kathleen R. McKeown and Dragomir R. Radev. 2000. Collocations. In Robert Dale, Hermann Moisl, and Harold Somers, editors, *A Handbook of Natural Language Processing*, pages 507–523. Marcel Dekker, New York, U.S.A.

I. Dan Melamed. 1997. A portable algorithm for mapping bitext correspondence. In *Proceedings of the 35th Conference of the Association for Computational Linguistics (ACL'97)*, pages 305–312, Madrid, Spain.

Igor Mel'čuk. 1998. Collocations and lexical functions. In Anthony P. Cowie, editor, *Phraseology. Theory, Analysis, and Applications*, pages 23–53. Claredon Press, Oxford.

Igor Mel'čuk. 2003. Collocations: définition, rôle et utilité. In Francis Grossmann and Agnès Tutin, editors, *Les collocations: analyse et traitement*, pages 23–32. Editions "De Werelt", Amsterdam.

Darren Pearce. 2001. Synonymy in collocation extraction. In *WordNet and Other Lexical Resources: Applications, Extensions and Customizations (NAACL 2001 Workshop)*, pages 41–46, Pittsburgh, U.S.A.

Pavel Pecina. 2005. An extensive empirical study of collocation extraction methods. In *Proceedings of the ACL Student Research Workshop*, pages 13–18, Ann Arbor, Michigan, June.

Ivan A. Sag, Timothy Baldwin, Francis Bond, Ann Copestake, and Dan Flickinger. 2002. Multiword expressions: A pain in the neck for NLP. In *Proceedings of the Third International Conference on Intelligent Text Processing and Computational Linguistics (CICLING 2002)*, pages 1–15, Mexico City.

Violeta Seretan and Eric Wehrli. 2006. Accurate collocation extraction using a multilingual parser. In *Proceedings of COLING/ACL 2006*. To appear.

Violeta Seretan, Luka Nerima, and Eric Wehrli. 2004. A tool for multi-word collocation extraction and visualization in multilingual corpora. In *Proceedings of the Eleventh EURALEX International Congress, EURALEX 2004*, pages 755–766, Lorient, France.

Violeta Seretan. 2005. Induction of syntactic collocation patterns from generic syntactic relations. In *Proceedings of Nineteenth International Joint Conference on Artificial Intelligence (IJCAI 2005)*, pages 1698–1699, Edinburgh, Scotland, July.

Sayori Shimohata, Toshiyuki Sugio, and Junji Nagata. 1997. Retrieving collocations by co-occurrences and word order constraints. In *Proceedings of the Annual Meeting of the Association for Computational Linguistics*, pages 476–481, Madrid, Spain.

John Sinclair. 1995. *Collins Cobuild English Dictionary*. Harper Collins, London.

Frank Smadja, Kathleen McKeown, and Vasileios Hatzivassiloglou. 1996. Translating collocations for bilingual lexicons: a statistical approach. *Computational Linguistics*, 22(1):1–38.

Frank Smadja. 1993. Retrieving collocations from text: Xtract. *Computational Linguistics*, 19(1):143–177.

Eric Wehrli. 2003. Translation of words in context. In *Proceedings of Machine Translation Summit IX*, pages 502–504, New Orleans, Lousiana, U.S.A.

Eric Wehrli. 2004. Un modèle multilingue d'analyse syntaxique. In A. Auchlin et al., editor, *Structures et discours - Mélanges offerts à Eddy Roulet*, pages 311–329. Éditions Nota bene, Québec.

Joachim Wermter and Udo Hahn. 2004. Collocation extraction based on modifiability statistics. In *Proceedings of the 20th International Conference on Computational Linguistics (COLING 2004)*, pages 980–986, Geneva, Switzerland.

Dekai Wu. 1994. Aligning a parallel English-Chinese corpus statistically with lexical criteria. In *Proceedings of the 32nd Annual Meeting of the Association for Computational Linguistics (ACL 1994)*, pages 80–87, Las Cruces (New Mexico), U.S.A.

Diana Zaiu Inkpen and Graeme Hirst. 2002. Acquiring collocations for lexical choice between near-synonyms. In *Proceedings of the ACL-02 Workshop on Unsupervised Lexical Acquisition*, pages 67–76, Philadephia, Pennsylvania.

Rémi Zajac, Elke Lange, and Jin Yang. 2003. Customizing complex lexical entries for high-quality MT. In *Proceedings of the Ninth Machine Translation Summit*, New Orleans, U.S.A.

Heike Zinsmeister and Ulrich Heid. 2003. Significant triples: Adjective+Noun+Verb combinations. In *Proceedings of the 7th Conference on Computational Lexicography and Text Research (Complex 2003), Budapest.*

Heike Zinsmeister and Ulrich Heid. 2004. Collocations of complex nouns: Evidence for lexicalisation. In *Proceedings of KONVENS 2004*, Vienna, Austria.

Structural properties of Lexical Systems: Monolingual and Multilingual Perspectives

Alain Polguère
OLST—Département de linguistique et de traduction
Université de Montréal
C.P. 6128, succ. Centre-ville, Montréal (Québec) H3C 3J7 Canada
alain.polguere@umontreal.ca

Abstract

We introduce a new type of lexical structure called *lexical system*, an interoperable model that can feed both monolingual and multilingual language resources. We begin with a formal characterization of lexical systems as "pure" directed graphs, solely made up of nodes corresponding to lexical entities and links. To illustrate our approach, we present data borrowed from a lexical system that has been generated from the French DiCo database. We later explain how the compilation of the original dictionary-like database into a net-like one has been made possible. Finally, we discuss the potential of the proposed lexical structure for designing multilingual lexical resources.

1 Introduction

The aim of this paper is to introduce, justify and exemplify a new type of structure for lexical resources called *lexical systems*. Although lexical systems are basically monolingual entities, we believe they are particularly well-suited for the implementation of interlingual connections.

Our demonstration of the value of lexical systems is centered around an experiment of lexical system generation that was performed using data tables extracted from the DiCo database of French paradigmatic and syntagmatic lexical links. This experiment has allowed us to produce a lexical system that is a richer structure than the original database it has been derived from.

In section 2, we characterize two main families of lexical databases presently available: dictionary-like *vs.* net-like lexical databases; we then proceed with describing the specific structure of lexical systems. Section 3 illustrates the functioning of lexical systems with data borrowed from the French DiCo database; this will show that lexical systems—that are basically net-like—are interoperable structures in respect to the information they can easily encode and the wide range of applications for which they can function as lexical resources. Section 4 describes how the generation of a lexical system from the French DiCo database has been implemented. Finally, in section 5, we address the problem of using lexical systems for feeding multilingual databases.

2 Structure of lexical systems

Lexical systems as formal models of natural language lexica are very much related to the "*-Net*" generation of lexical databases, whose most well-known representatives are undoubtedly WordNet (Fellbaum, 1998) and FrameNet (Baker *et al.*, 2003). However, lexical systems possess some very specific characteristics that clearly distinguish them from other lexicographic structures. We will first characterize the two main current approaches to the structuring of lexical models and then present lexical systems relative to them.

2.1 Dictionary- vs. net-like lexical databases

Dictionary-like databases as texts

The most straightforward way of building lexical databases is to use standard dictionaries (i.e. books) and turn them into electronic entities. It is the approach taken by most publishing companies (e.g. American Heritage (2000)), with various degrees of sophistication. Resulting products

Proceedings of the Workshop on Multilingual Language Resources and Interoperability, pages 50–59,
Sydney, July 2006.

can be termed *dictionary-like databases*. They are mainly characterized by two features.

- They are made up of word (word sense) descriptions, called *dictionary entries*.
- Dictionary entries can be seen as "texts," in the most general sense.

Consequently, dictionary-like databases are before all huge texts, consisting of a collection of much smaller texts (i.e. entries).

It seems natural to consider electronic versions of standard dictionaries as texts. However, formal lexical databases such as the multilingual XML-based JMDict (Breen, 2004) are also textual in nature. There are collections of entries, each entry consisting of a structured text that "tells us something" about a word. Even databases encoding relational models of the lexicon can be 100% textual, and therefore dictionary-like. Such is the case of the French DiCo database (Polguère, 2000), that we have used for compiling our lexical system. As we will see later, the original DiCo database is nothing but a collection of lexicographic records, each record being subdivided into fields that are basically small texts. Although the DiCo is built within the framework of Explanatory Combinatorial Lexicology (Mel'čuk *et al.*, 1995) and concentrates on the description of lexical links, it is clearly not designed as a "*-Net*" database, in the sense of WordNet or FrameNet.

Net-like databases as graphs

Most lexical models, even standard dictionaries, are relational in nature. For instance, all dictionaries define words in terms of other words, use pointers such as 'Synonym' and 'Antonym.' However, their structure does not reflect their relational nature. The situation is totally different with true net-like databases. They can be characterized as follows.

- They are graphs—huge sets of connected entities—rather than collections of small texts (entries).
- They are not necessarily centered around words, or word senses. They use as nodes a potentially heterogeneous set of lexical or, more generally, linguistic entities.

Net-like databases are, for many, the most suitable knowledge structures for modeling lexica. Nevertheless, databases such as WordNet pose one major problem: they are inherently structured according to a couple of hierarchizing and/or classifying principles. WordNet, for instance, is semantically-oriented and imposes a hierarchical organization of lexical entities based, first of all, on two specific semantic relations: synonymy—through the grouping of lexical meanings within *synsets*—and hypernymy. Additionally, the part of speech classification of lexical units creates a strict partition of the database: WordNet is made up of four separate synset hierarchies (for nouns, verbs, adjectives and adverbs). We do not believe lexical models should be designed following a few rigid principles that impose a hierarchization or classification of data. Such structuring is of course extremely useful, even necessary, but should be projected "on demand" onto lexical models. Furthermore, there should not be a predefined, finite set of potential structuring principles; data structures should welcome any of them, and this is precisely one of the main characteristics of lexical systems, that will be presented shortly (section 2.2).

Texts *vs.* graphs: pros and cons

It is essential to stress the fact that any dictionary-like database can be turned into a net-like database and vice versa. Of course, dictionary-like databases that rely on relational models are more compatible with graph encoding. However, there are always relational data in dictionaries, and such data can be extracted and "reformatted" in the form of nodes and connecting links.

The important issue is therefore not one of exclusive choice between the two types of structures; it concerns what each structure is better at. In our opinion, the specialization of each type of structure is as follows.

Dictionary-like structures are tools for editing (writing) and consulting lexical information. Linguistic intuition of lexicographers or users of lexical models performs best on texts. Both lexicographers and users need to be able to see the whole picture about words, and need the entry format at a certain stage—although other ways of displaying lexical information, such as tables, are extremely useful too![1]

Net-like structures are tools for implementing dynamic aspects of lexica: wading through lexical knowledge, adding to it, revising it or infer-

[1] It is no coincidence if WordNet so-called *lexicographer files* give a textual perspective on lexical items that is quite dictionary-like. The unit of description is the synset, however, and not the lexical unit. (See WordNet on-line documentation on lexicographer files.)

ring information from it. Consequently, net-like databases are believed by some (and we share this opinion) to have some form of cognitive validity. They are compatible with observations made, for instance, in Aitchison (2003) on the network nature of the mental lexicon. Last but not least, net-like databases can more easily integrate other lexical structures or be integrated by them.

In conclusion, although both forms of structures are compatible at a certain level and have their own advantages in specific contexts of use, we are particularly interested by the fact that net-like databases are more prone to live an "organic life" in terms of evolution (addition, subtraction, replacement) and interaction with other data structures (connection with models of other languages, with grammars, etc.).

2.2 Lexical systems: a new type of net-like lexical databases

As mentioned above, most net-like lexical databases seem to focus on the description of just a few properties of natural language lexica (quasi-synonymy, hypernymic organization of word senses, predicative structures and their syntactic expression, etc.). Consequently, developers of these databases often have to gradually "stretch" their models in order to add the description of new types of phenomena, that were not of primary concern at the onset. It is legitimate to expect that such graft of new components will leave scars on the initial design of lexical models.

The lexical structures we propose, lexical systems (hereafter *LS*), do not pose this type of problem for two reasons.

First, they are not oriented towards the modeling of just a few specific lexical phenomena, but originate from a global vision of the lexicon as central component of linguistic knowledge.

Second, they have a very simple, flat organization, that does not impose any hierarchical or classifying structure on the lexicon. Let us explain how it works.

The design of any given LS has to follow four basic principles, that cannot be tampered with: LSs are 1) pure directed graphs, 2) non-hierarchical, 3) heterogeneous and 4) equipped for modeling fuzziness of lexical knowledge. We will briefly examine each of these principles.

Pure directed graph. An LS is a directed graph, and just that. This means that, from a formal point of view, it is **uniquely** made up of nodes and oriented links connecting these nodes.

Non hierarchical. An LS is a non-hierarchical structure, although it can contain sets of nodes that are hierarchically connected. For instance, we will see later that the DiCo LS contains nodes that correspond to a hierarchically organized set of semantic labels. The hierarchy of DiCo semantic labels can be used to project a structured perspective on the LS; but the LS itself is by no means organized according to one or more specific hierarchies.

Heterogeneous. An LS is a potentially heterogeneous collection of nodes. Three main families of nodes can be found:

- genuine lexical entities such as lexemes, idioms, wordforms, etc.;
- quasi-lexical entities, such as collocations, lexical functions,[2] free expressions worth storing in the lexicon (e.g. "canned" linguistic examples), etc.;
- lexico-grammatical entities, such as syntactic patterns of expression of semantic actants, grammatical features, etc.

Prototypical LS nodes are first of all lexical entities, but we have to expect LSs to contain as nodes entities that do not strictly belong to the lexicon: they can belong to the interface between the lexicon and the grammar of the language. Such is the case of subcategorization frames, called *government patterns* in Explanatory Combinatorial Lexicology. As rules specifying patterns of syntactic structures, they belong to the grammar of the language. However, as preassembled constructs on which lexemes "sit" in sentences, they are clearly closer to the lexical realm of the language than rules for building passive sentences or handling agreements, for instance.

With fuzziness. Each component of an LS, whether node or link, carries a trust value, i.e. a measure of its validity. Clearly, there are many ways of attributing and handling trust values in order to implement fuzziness in knowledge structures. For instance, in our experiments with the DiCo LS, we have adopted a simplistic approach, that was satisfactory for our present needs but should become more elaborate as we proceed with developing and using LSs. In our present implementation, we make use of only three possible trust values: "`1`" means that as far as we can tell—i.e. trusting what is explicitly asserted in the DiCo—the information is correct; "`0.5`" means

[2] On collocations and lexical functions, see section 3 below.

that the corresponding information is the result of an inference made from the input data and was not explicitly asserted by lexicographers; "0" means that the information ought to be incorrect—for instance, in case we identified a bogus lexical pointer in data imported from the DiCo.

Fuzziness encoding is an essential feature of LSs, as structures on which inference can take place or as structures that are, at least partially, inferred from others (in case of generation of LSs from existing lexical databases). Of course, any trust value is not absolute. "1" does not mean the information is valid no matter what, and "0" that it is necessarily false. Information in LSs, and the rating of this information, is no more absolute than any information that may be stored in someone's mental lexicon. However, if we want to compute on LSs' content, it is essential to be able to distinguish between data we have all reasons to believe to be true and data we have all reasons to believe to be false. As a matter of fact, this feature of LSs has helped us in two ways while compiling the DiCo LS: (i) we were able to infer new descriptions from data contained in the original DiCo while keeping track of the inferred nature of this new information (that ought to be validated); (ii) we kept record of incoherences found in the DiCo by attributing a trust value of 0 to the corresponding elements in the LS.

It is now high time to give concrete examples of LS data. But before we proceed, let us emphasize the fact that no other formal devices than those that have just been introduced are allowed in LSs. Anything else we may want to add must be relevant to other components of the linguistic model, to the grammar for instance. Notice, however, that we do not exclude the need to add a measure of the relative "weight" of nodes and links. This measure, different from the trust value, would reflect the degree of activation of each LS element. For instance, the DiCo entry for DÉFAITE 'defeat' lists quite a few support verbs that take this noun as complement, among which CONNAÎTRE 'to know' and SUBIR 'to suffer.' Weight values could indicate that the former verb is much less commonly used than the second in this context. Another advantage of weight is that it could help optimize navigation through the LS graph, when several paths can be taken.

3 Examples borrowed from the DiCo LS

The DiCo is a French lexical database that focuses on the modeling of paradigmatic and syntagmatic lexical links controlled by lexical units. Paradigmatic links correspond to so-called *semantic derivations* (synonymy, antonymy, nominalization, verbalization, names for actants or typical circonstants, etc.). Syntagmatic links corresponds to collocations controlled by lexical units (intensifiers, support verbs, etc.). These lexical properties are encoded by means of a system of metalexical entities known as *lexical functions*. (For a presentation of the system of lexical functions, see Mel'čuk (1996) and Kahane and Polguère (2001).) Although it does not contain actual definitions, the DiCo partially describes the semantic content of each lexical unit with two formal tools: (i) a semantic label, that corresponds to the genus (core component) of the lexical unit's definition and (ii) a "propositional formula," which states the predicative nature of the unit (non-predicative meaning or predicate with one, two or more arguments). Each entry also gives the government pattern (roughly, the subcategorization frame) of the unit and lists idioms (phrasal lexical units) that contain the unit under description. Finally, each entry contains a set of examples retrieved from corpora or the Internet. As one can see, the DiCo covers a fairly large range of lexical properties; for more information on the DiCo, one can refer to Polguère (2000) and Lareau (2002).

Presently, the DiCo is developed as a FileMaker® database. Each DiCo entry corresponds to a record in the database, and the core of each record is the field that contains lexical function links controlled by the *headword* (i.e. the lexical unit described in the entry). Data in (1) below is one item in the lexical function field of the DiCo record for Fr. RANCUNE ('resentment'):

(1)
```
        /*[X] éprouver ~*/
    {Oper12} avoir, éprouver, nourrir,
             ressentir
             [ART ~ Prép-envers N=Y]
```

We isolate five different types of LS entities in the above example:

- The expression between curly brackets `Oper12` is the name of a lexical function denoting a type of support verbs.[3]
- `{Oper12}` as a whole denotes `Oper12`(RANCUNE), the application of

[3] More precisely, `Oper12` denotes support verbs that take the 1st actant of the headword as subject, the headword itself as 1st complement and the 2nd actant of the headword as 2nd complement; for instance: *X **feels**/**has** resentment for Y.*

the `Oper12` lexical function to its argument (the headword of the entry).

- The preceding formula—between the two /*...*/ symbols—is a gloss for `Oper12`(RANCUNE). This metalinguistic encoding of the content of the lexical function application is for the benefit of users who do not master the system of lexical functions.
- Following the name of the lexical function is the list of values of the lexical function application, each of which is a specific lexical entity. In this case, they are all collocates of the headword, due to the syntagmatic nature of `Oper12`.
- Finally, the expression between square brackets is the description of the syntactic structure controlled by the collocates. It corresponds to a special case of lexico-grammatical entities mentioned earlier in section 2.2. These entities have not been processed yet in our LS and they will be ignored in the discussion below.

Data in (1) corresponds to a very small subgraph in the generated LS, which is visualized in Figure 1 below. Notice that graphical representations we used here have been automatically generated in GraphML format from the LS and then displayed with the yEd graph editor/viewer.

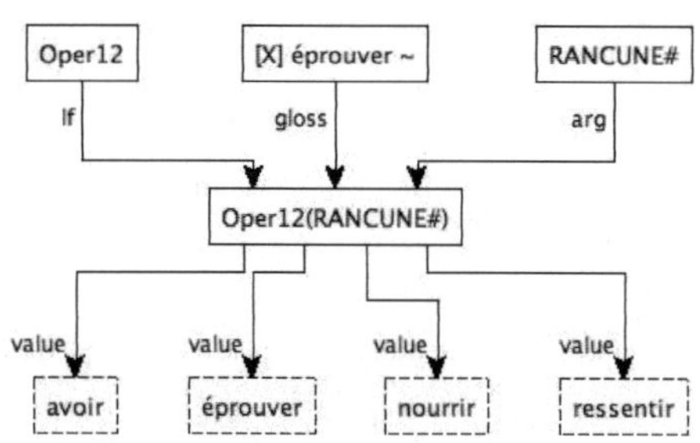

Figure 1. LS interpretation of (1)

This graph shows how DiCo data given in (1) have been modeled in terms of lexical entities and links. We see that lexical function applications are lexical entities: something to be communicated, that is pointing to actual means of expressing it. The argument (`arg` link) of the lexical function application, the lexical unit RANCUNE, is of course also a lexical entity (although of a different nature). The same holds for the values (`value` links). None of these values, however, has been diagnosed as possessing a corresponding entry in the DiCo. Consequently, the compilation process has given them the (temporary) status of simple wordforms, with a trust value of `0.5`, visualized here by boxes with hashed borders. (Continuous lines for links or boxes indicate a trust value of `1`.) Ultimately, it will be the task of lexicographers to add to the DiCo entries for the corresponding senses of AVOIR, ÉPROUVER, NOURRIR and RESSENTIR.

One may be surprised to see lexical functions (such as `Oper1`) appear as lexical entities in our LS, because of their very "abstract" nature. Two facts justify this approach. First, lexical units too are rather abstract entities. While wordforms *horse* and *horses* could be considered as more "concrete," their grouping under a label *HORSE lexical unit* is not a trivial abstraction. Second, lexical functions are not only descriptive tools in Explanatory Combinatorial Lexicology. They are also conceptualized as generalization of lexical units that play an important role text production, in general rules of paraphrase for instance.

This first illustration demonstrates how the LS version of the DiCo reflects its true relational nature, contrary to its original dictionary-like format as a FileMaker database. It also shows how varied lexical entities can be and how trust values can help keep track of the distinction between what has been explicitly stated by lexicographers and what can be inferred from what they stated.

The next illustration will build on the first one and show how so-called *non-standard lexical functions* are integrated into the LS. Until now, we have been referring only to standard lexical functions, i.e. lexical functions that belong to the small universal core of lexical relations identified in Explanatory Combinatorial Lexicology (or, more generally, in Meaning-Text theory). However, all paradigmatic and syntagmatic links are not necessarily standard. Here is an illustration, borrowed from the DiCo entry for CHAT 'cat'.

(2)
```
{Ce qu'on dit
 pour appeler ~} « Minet ! »,
                 « Minou ! »,
                 « Petit ! »
```

Here, a totally non-standard lexical function `Ce qu'on dit pour appeler ~` 'What one says to call ~ [= a cat]' has been used to connect the headword CHAT to expressions such as *Minou !* 'Kitty kitty!' As one can see, no gloss has been introduced, because non-standard lexical functions are already explicit, non-formal encoding of lexical relations. The LS interpretation of (2) is therefore a simpler structure than the one used in our previous illustration, as shown in Figure 2.

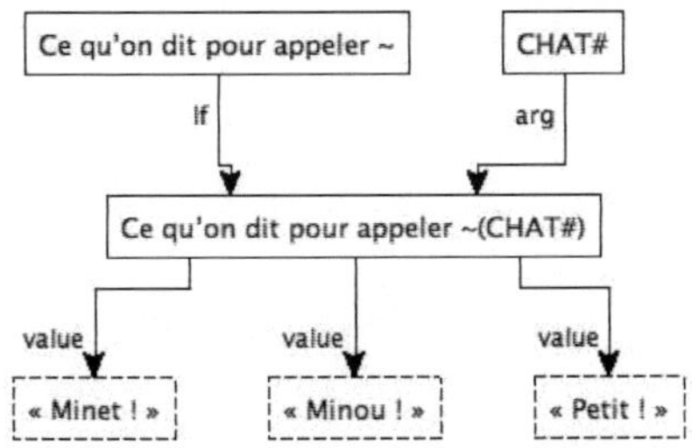

Figure 2. LS interpretation of (2)

Our last illustration will show how it is possible to project a hierarchical structuring on the DiCo LS when, **and only when**, it is needed.

The hierarchy of semantic labels used to semantically characterize lexical units in the DiCo has been compiled into the DiCo LS together with the lexical database proper. Each semantic label is connected to its more generic label or labels (as this hierarchy allows for multiple inheritance) with an `is_a` link. Additionally, it is connected to the lexical units it labels by `label` links. It is thus possible to simply pull the hierarchy of semantic labels out of the LS and it will "fish out" all lexical units of the LS, hierarchically organized through hypernymy. Notice that this is different from extracting from the DiCo all lexical units that possess a specific semantic label: we extract all units **whose semantic label belongs to a given subhierarchy** in the system of semantic labels. Figure 3 below is the graphical result of pulling the `accessoire` ('accessory') subhierarchy.

To avoid using labels on links, we have programmed the generation of this class of GraphML structures with links encoded as follows: `is_a` links (between semantic labels) appear as thick continuous arrows and `label` links (between semantic labels and lexical units they label) as thin dotted arrows.

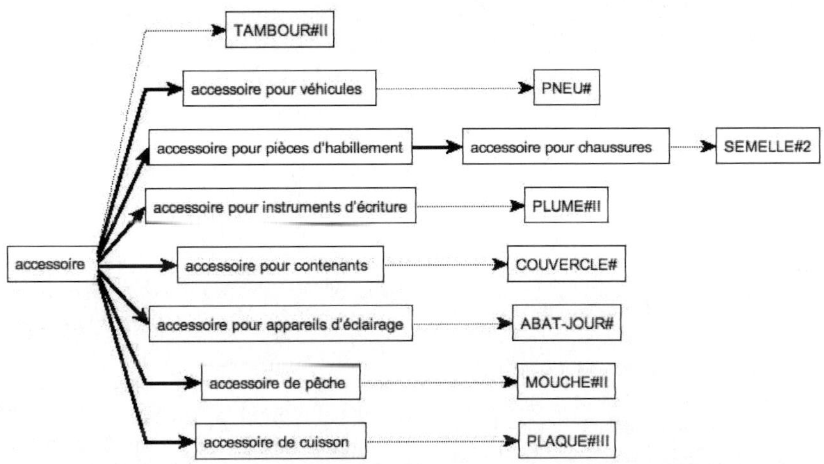

Figure 3. The `accessoire` ('accessory') semantic subhierarchy in the DiCo LS

The "beauty" of LSs' structuring does not lie in the fact that it allows us to automatically generate fancy graphical representations. Such representations are just a convenient way to make explicit the internal structure of LSs. What really interests us is what can be done with LSs once we consider them from a **functional** perspective.

The main functional advantage of LSs lies in the fact that these structures are both cannibal and prone to be cannibalized. Let us explain the two facets of this somehow gruesome metaphor.

First, directed graphs are powerful structures that can encode virtually any kind of information and are particularly suited for lexical knowledge. If one believes that a lexicon is before all a relational entity, we can postulate that all information present in any form of dictionary and database can eventually be compiled into LS structures. The experiment we did in compiling the DiCo (see details in section 4) demonstrates well enough this property of LS structures.

Second, because of their extreme simplicity, LS structures can conversely always be "digested" by other, more specific types of structures, such as XML versions of dictionary- or net-like databases. For instance, we have regenerated from our LS a DiCo in HTML format, with hyperlinks for entry cross-references and color-coding for trust values of linguistic information. Interestingly, this HTML by-product of the LS contains entries that do not exist in the original DiCo. They are produced for each value of lexical function applications that does not correspond to an entry in the DiCo. The content of these entries is made up of "inverse" lexical function relations: pointers to lexical function applications for which the lexical entity is a value. These new entries can be seen as rough drafts, that can be used by lexicographers to write new entries. We will provide more details of this at the end of the next section.

4 Compiling the DiCo (dictionary-like) database into a lexical system

The DiCo is presently available both in FileMaker format and as SQL tables, accessible through the DiCouèbe interface.[4] It is these tables that are used as input for the generation of LSs.[5] They present the advantage of being the result of an extensive processing of the DiCo that splits its content into elementary pieces of lexicographic information (Steinlin *et al.*, 2005). It is therefore quite easy to analyze them further in order to perform a restructuring in terms of LS modeling.

The task of inferring new information, information that is not explicitly encoded in the DiCo, is the delicate part of the compilation process, due to the richness of the database. Until now, we have only implemented a small subset of all inferences that can be made. For instance, we have inferred individual lexemes from idioms that appear inside DiCo records (COUP DE SOLEIL 'sunburn' entails the probable existence of the three lexemes COUP, DE and SOLEIL). We have also distinguished lexical entities that are actual lexical units from their signifiers (linguistic forms). Signifiers, which do not have to be associated with one specific meaning, play an important role when it comes to wading through an LS (for instance, when we want to separate word access through form and through meaning).

We cannot give here all details of the compilation process. Suffice it to say that, at the present stage, some important information contained in the DiCo is not processed yet. For instance, we have not implemented the compilation of government patterns and lexicographic examples. On the other hand, all lexical function applications and the semantic labeling of lexical units are properly handled. Recall that we import together with the DiCo a hierarchy of semantic labels used by the DiCo lexicographers, which allows us to establish hypernymic links between lexical units, as shown in Figure 3 above.[6] Codewise, the DiCo LS is just a flat Prolog database with clauses for only two predicates:

```
entity( <Numerical ID>, <Name>,
        <Type>, <Trust> )
link( <Numerical ID>, <Source ID>,
      <Target ID>, <Type>, <Trust> )
```

Here are some statistics on the content of the DiCo LS at the time of writing.

Nodes : **37,808**

780 semantic labels; **1,301** vocables (= entries in the "LS wordlist"); **1,690** lexical units (= senses of vocables); **6,464** wordforms; **2,268** non lexicalized expressions; **7,389** monolexical signifiers; **948** multilexical signifiers; **3,443** lexical functions; **9,417** lexical function applications; **4,108** glosses of lexical function applications

Links : **61,714**

871 "is_a," between semantic labels; **775** "sem_label," between sem. labels and lexical units; **1,690** "sense," between vocables and lexical units corresponding to specific senses; **2,991** "basic_form," between mono- or multilexical signifiers and vocables or lexical units; **6,464** "signifier," between wordforms and monolexical signifiers; **4,135** "used_in," between monolexical signifiers and multiliexical signifiers; **9,417** "lf," between lexical functions and their application; **6,064** "gloss," between lex. func. appl. and their gloss; **9,417** "arg," between lex. func. appl. and their argument; **19,890** "value," between lex. func. appl. and each of the value elements they return

Let us make a few comments on these numbers in order to illustrate how the generation of the LS from the original DiCo database works.

The FileMaker (or SQL) DiCo database that has been used contained only 775 lexical unit records (word senses). This is reflected in statistics by the number of `sem_label` links between semantic labels and lexical units: only lexical units that were headwords of DiCo records possess a semantic labeling. Statistics above show that the LS contains 1,690 lexical units. So where do the 915 (1,690 – 775) extra units come from? They all have been extrapolated from the so-called phraseology (`ph`) field of DiCo records, where lexicographers list idioms that are formally built from the record headword. For instance, the DiCo record for BARBE 'beard' contained (among others) a pointer to the idiom BARBE À PAPA 'cotton candy.' This idiom did not possess its own record in the original DiCo and has been "reified"

[4] http://www.olst.umontreal.ca/dicouebe.

[5] The code for compiling the DiCo into an LS, generating GraphML exports and generating an HTML version of the DiCo has been written in SWI-Prolog.

[6] The hierarchy of semantic labels is developed with the Protégé ontology editor. We use XML exports from Protégé to inject this hierarchy inside the LS. This is another illustration of the cannibalistic (and not too choosy) nature of LSs.

while generating the LS, among 914 other idioms.

The "wordlist" of our LS is therefore much more developed than the wordlist of the DiCo it is derived from. This is particularly true if we include in it the 6,464 wordform entities. As explained earlier, it is possible to regenerate from the LS lexical descriptions for any lexical entity that is either a lexical unit or a wordform targeted by a lexical function application, filling wordform descriptions with inverse lexical function links. To test this, we have regenerated an entire DiCo in HTML format from the LS, with a total of 8,154 (1,690 + 6,464) lexical entries, stored as individual HTML pages. Pages for original DiCo headwords contain the hypertext specification of the original lexical function links, together with all inverse lexical links that have been found in the LS; pages for wordforms contain only inverse links. For instance, the page for METTRE 'to put' (which is not a headword in the original DiCo) contains 71 inverse links, such as:[7]

```
CausOper1( À L'ARRIÈRE-PLAN# ) ->
Labor12( ACCUSATION#I.2 ) ->
Caus1[1]Labreal1( ANCRE# ) ->
Labor21( ANGOISSE# ) ->
Labreal12( ARMOIRE# ) ->
```

Of course, most of the entries that were not in the original DiCo are fairly poor and will require significant editing to be turned into *bona fide* DiCo descriptions. They are, however, a useful point of departure for lexicographers; additionally, the richer the DiCo will become, the more productive the LS will be in terms of automatic generation of draft descriptions.

5 Lexical systems and multilinguality

The approach to multilingual implementation of lexical resources that LSs allow is compatible with strategies used in known multilingual databases, such as Papillon (Sérasset and Mangeot-Lerebours, 2001): it sees multilingual resources as connections of basically monolingual models. In this final section, we first argue for a monolingual perspective on the problem of multilinguality. We then make proposals for implementing interlingual connections by means of LSs.

[7] We underline hypertext links. Lexical function applications listed here correspond French collocations that mean, respectively, *to put in the background*, *to indict someone* (literally in French 'to put someone in accusation'), *to anchor a vessel* (literally in French 'to put a vessel at the anchor'), *to put someone in anguish*, *to keep something in a cupboard.*

5.1 Theoretical and methodological primacy of monolingual structures

We see two logical reasons why the issue of designing multilingual lexical databases should be tackled from a monolingual perspective.

First, all natural languages can perfectly well be conceived of in complete isolation. In fact, monolingual speakers are no less "true" speakers of a language than multilingual speakers.

Second, acquisition of multiple languages commonly takes place in situations where **second** languages are acquired as additions to an already mastered first language. Multiplicity in linguistic competence is naturally implemented by graft of a language on top of a preexisting linguistic knowledge. How multiple lexica are acquired and stored is a much debated issue (Schreuder and Weltens, 1993), which is outside the scope of our research. However, it is now commonly accepted that even children who are bilingual "from birth" develop two linguistic systems, each of which being quite similar in essence to linguistic systems of monolingual speakers (de Houwer, 1990). The main issue is thus one of systems' connectivity.

From a theoretical and practical point of view, it is thus perfectly legitimate to see the problem of structuring multilingual resources as one of, first, finding the most adequate and interoperable structuring for monolingual resources. This being said, we do not believe that the issue of structuring monolingual databases has already been dealt with once and for all in a satisfactory manner. We hope the concept of LS we introduce here will stimulate reflection on that topic.

5.2 Multilingual connections between LSs

A multilingual lexical resource based on the LS architecture should be made up of several **fully autonomous LSs**, i.e., LSs that are not specially tailored for multilingual connections. They should function as independent modules that can be connected while preserving their integrity.

Connections between LSs should be implemented as specialized interlingual links between equivalent lexical entities. There is one exception however: standard lexical functions (`A1`, `Magn`, `AntiMagn`, `Oper1`, etc.). Because they are universal lexical entities, they should be stored in a specialized interlingual module; as universals, they play a central role in interlingual connectivity (Fontenelle, 1997). However, these are only "pure" lexical functions. Lexical function applications, such as `Oper12`(RANCUNE) above, are by no means universals and have to be connected to their counterpart in other languages. Let us examine briefly this aspect of the question.

One has to distinguish at least two main cases of interlingual lexical connections in LSs: direct lexical connections and connections through lexical function applications.

Direct connections, such as Fr. RANCUNE *vs.* Eng. RESENTMENT should be implemented—manually or using existing bilingual resources—as simple interlingual (i.e. intermodule) links between two lexical entities. Things are not always that simple though, due to the existence of partial or multiple interlingual connections. For instance, what interlingual link should originate from Eng. SIBLING if we want to point to a French counterpart? As there is no lexicalized French equivalent, we may be tempted to include in the French LS entities such as *frère ou sœur* ('brother or sister'). We have two strong objections to this. First, this complex entity will not be a proper translation in most contexts: one cannot translate *He killed all his siblings* by *Il a tué tous ses frères ou sœurs*—the conjunction *et* 'and' is required in this specific context, as well as in many others. Second, and this is more problematic, this approach would force us to enter in the French LS entities for translation purposes, which would transgress the original monolingual integrity of the system.[8] We must admit that we do not have a ready-to-use solution to this problem, specially if we insist on ruling out the introduction of *ad hoc* periphrastic translations as lexical entities in target LSs. It may very well be the case that a cluster of interrelated LSs cannot be completely connected for translation purposes without the addition of "buffer" LSs that ensure full interlingual connectivity. For instance, the buffer French LS for English to French LS connection could contain phrasal lexical entities such as *frères et sœurs* ('siblings'), *être de mêmes parents* and *être frère*(*s*) et *sœur*(*s*) ('to be siblings'). This strategy can actually be very productive and can lead us to realize that what appeared first as an *ad hoc* solution may be fully justified from a linguistic perspective. Dealing with the *sibling* case, for instance, forced us to realized that while *frère*(*s*) *et sœur*(*s*) sounds very normal in French, *sœur*(*s*) *et frère*(*s*) will seem odd or, at least, intentionally built that way. This is a very strong argument for considering that a lexical entity (we do not say *lexical unit*!) *frère*(*s*) *et sœur*(*s*) **does** exist in French, independently from the translation problem that *sibling* poses to us. This phrasal entity should probably be present in any complete French LS.

The case of connections through lexical function applications is even trickier. A simplistic approach would be to consider that it is sufficient to connect interlinguistically lexical function applications to get all resulting lexical connections for value elements. For standard lexical functions, this can be done automatically using the following strategy for two languages A and B.

> If the lexical entity L_A is connected to L_B by means of a "translation" link,
> all lexical entities linked to the lexical function application **f**(L_A) by the "value" link should be connected by a "value translation" link, with a trust value of "0.5," to all lexical entities linked to **f**(L_B) by a "value" link.

The distinction between "translation" and "value translation" links allow for contextual interlingual connections: a lexical entity L'_B could happen to be a proper translation of L'_A only if it occurs as collocate in a specific collocation. But this is not enough. It is also necessary to filter "value translation" connections that are systematically generated using the above strategy. For instance, each of the specific values given in (1) section 3 should be associated with its **closest** equivalent among values of **`Oper12`**(RESENTMENT): HAVE, FEEL, HARBOR, NOURISH, etc. At the present time, we do not see how this can be achieved automatically, unless we can make use of already available multilingual databases of collocations. For English and French, for instance, we plan to experiment in the near future with T. Fontenelle's database of English-French collocation pairs (Fontenelle, 1997). These collocations have been extracted from the *Collins-Robert* dictionary and manually indexed by means of lexical functions. We are convinced it is possible to use this database firstly to build a first version of a new English LS and, secondly, to implement the type fine-grained multilingual connections between lexical function values illustrated with our RANCUNE *vs.* RESENTMENT example.

We are well aware that we have probably surfaced as many problems as we have offered solutions in this section. However, the above considerations show at least two things:

---

[8] It is worth noticing that good English-French dictionaries, such as the *Collins-Robert*, offer several different translations in this particular case. Additionally, their translations do not apply to *sibling* as such, but rather to *siblings* or to expressions such as *someone's siblings*, *to be siblings*, etc.

- LSs have the merit to make explicit the scale of the problem of interlingual lexical correspondence, if one want to tackle this problem in a fine-grained manner;[9]
- the implementation of multilingual connections over LSs should be approached using semi-automatic strategies.

6 Conclusions

We have achieved the production of a significant LS, which can be considered of broad coverage in terms of the sheer number of entities and links it contains and the richness of linguistic knowledge it encodes. We plan to finish the absorption of all information contained in the dictionary-like DiCo (including information that can be inferred). We also want to integrate complementary French databases into the LS (for instance the Morphalou database,[10] for morphological information) and start to implement multilingual connections using T. Fontenelle's collocation database. Another development will be the construction of an editor to access and modify the content of our LS. This tool could also be used to develop DiCo-style LSs for other languages than French.

Acknowledgments

This research is supported by the *Fonds québécois de la recherche sur la Société et la culture* (FQRSC). We are very grateful to Sylvain Kahane, Marie-Claude L'Homme, Igor Mel'čuk, Ophélie Tremblay and four MLRI 2006 anonymous reviewers for their comments on a preliminary version of this paper. A very special thank to Sylvain Kahane and Jacques Steinlin for their invaluable work on the DiCo SQL, that made our own research possible.

References

American Heritage. 2000. *The American Heritage Dictionary of the English Language.* Fourth Edition, CD-ROM, Houghton Mifflin, Boston, MA.

Jean Aitchison. 2003. *Words in the Mind: An Introduction to the Mental Lexicon*, 3rd edition, Blackwell, Oxford, UK.

Collin F. Baker, Charles J. Fillmore and Beau Cronin. 2003. The Structure of the Framenet Database. *Int. Journal of Lexicography*, 16(3): 281-296.

James W. Breen. 2004. JMdict: a Japanese-Multilingual Dictionary. *Proceedings of COLING Multilingual Linguistic Resources Workshop*, Geneva, Switzerland.

Annick de Houwer. 1990. *The Acquisition of Two Languages from Birth. A Case Study*, Cambridge University Press, Cambridge, UK.

Christiane Fellbaum. 1998. *WordNet: An Electronic Lexical Database*, MIT Press, Cambridge, MA.

Thierry Fontenelle. 1997. *Turning a bilingual dictionary into a lexical-semantic database*, Niemeyer, Tübingen, Germany.

Sylvain Kahane and Alain Polguère. 2001. Formal foundation of lexical functions. *Proceedings of ACL/EACL 2001 Workshop on Collocation*, Toulouse, France, 8-15.

François Lareau. 2002. A Practical Guide for Writing DiCo Entries. *Third Papillon 2002 Seminar*, Tokyo, Japan [http://www.papillon-dictionary.org/Consult-Informations.po?docid=1620757&docLang=eng].

Igor Mel'čuk. 1996. Lexical Functions: A Tool for the Description of Lexical Relations in the Lexicon. In Leo Wanner (ed.): *Lexical Functions in Lexicography and Natural Language Processing*, Amsterdam/ Philadelphia: Benjamins, 37-102.

Igor Mel'čuk, André Clas and Alain Polguère. 1995. *Introduction à la lexicologie explicative et combinatoire*, Duculot, Louvain-la-Neuve, Belgium.

Igor Mel'čuk and Leo Wanner. 2001. Towards a Lexicographic Approach to Lexical Transfer in Machine Translation (Illustrated by the German-Russian Language Pair). *Machine Translation*, 16: 21-87.

Alain Polguère. 2000. Towards a theoretically-motivated general public dictionary of semantic derivations and collocations for French. *Proceedings of EURALEX'2000*, Stuttgart, Germany, 517-527.

Robert Schreuder and Bert Weltens (eds.). 1993. *The Bilingual lexicon*, Amsterdam, Benjamins.

Gilles Sérasset and Mathieu Mangeot-Lerebours. 2001. Papillon lexical database project: Monolingual dictionaries and interlingual links. *Proceedings of the 6th Natural Language Processing Pacific Rim Symposium*, Tokyo, Japan, 119–125.

Jacques Steinlin, Sylvain Kahane and Alain Polguère. 2005. Compiling a "classical" explanatory combinatorial lexicographic description into a relational database. *Proceedings of the Second International Conference on the Meaning Text Theory*, Moscow, Russia, 477-485.

[9] For a systematic analysis of interlingual lexical correspondences, see Mel'čuk and Wanner (2001).

[10] http://actarus.atilf.fr/morphalou/

A fast and accurate method for detecting English-Japanese parallel texts

Ken'ichi Fukushima, Kenjiro Taura and Takashi Chikayama
University of Tokyo
ken@tkl.iis.u-tokyo.ac.jp
{tau,chikayama}@logos.ic.i.u-tokyo.ac.jp

Abstract

Parallel corpus is a valuable resource used in various fields of multilingual natural language processing. One of the most significant problems in using parallel corpora is the lack of their availability. Researchers have investigated approaches to collecting parallel texts from the Web. A basic component of these approaches is an algorithm that judges whether a pair of texts is parallel or not. In this paper, we propose an algorithm that accelerates this task without losing accuracy by preprocessing a bilingual dictionary as well as the collection of texts. This method achieved 250,000 pairs/sec throughput on a single CPU, with the best F_1 score of 0.960 for the task of detecting 200 Japanese-English translation pairs out of $40,000$. The method is applicable to texts of any format, and not specific to HTML documents labeled with URLs. We report details of these preprocessing methods and the fast comparison algorithm. To the best of our knowledge, this is the first reported experiment of extracting Japanese–English parallel texts from a large corpora based solely on linguistic content.

1 Introduction

"Parallel text" is a pair of texts which is written in different languages and is a translation of each other. A compilation of parallel texts offered in a serviceable form is called a "parallel corpus". Parallel corpora are very valuable resources in various fields of multilingual natural language processing such as statistical machine translation (Brown et al., 1990), cross-lingual IR (Chen and Nie, 2000), and construction of dictionary (Nagao, 1996).

However, it is generally difficult to obtain parallel corpora of enough quantity and quality. There have only been a few varieties of parallel corpora. In addition, their languages have been biased toward English–French and their contents toward official documents of governmental institutions or software manuals. Therefore, it is often difficult to find a parallel corpus that meets the needs of specific researches.

To solve this problem, approaches to collect parallel texts from the Web have been proposed. In the Web space, all sorts of languages are used though English is dominating, and the content of the texts seems to be as diverse as all activities of the human-beings. Therefore, this approach has a potential to break the limitation in the use of parallel corpora.

Previous works successfully built parallel corpora of interesting sizes. Most of them utilized URL strings or HTML tags as a clue to efficiently find parallel documents (Yang and Li, 2002; Nadeau and Foster, 2004). Depending on such information specific to webpages limits the applicability of the methods. Even for webpages, many parallel texts not conforming to the presupposed styles will be left undetected. In this work, we have therefore decided to focus on a generally applicable method, which is solely based on the textual content of the documents. The main challenge then is how to make judgements fast.

Our proposed method utilizes a bilingual dictionary which, for each word in tne language, gives the list of translations in the other. The method preprocesses both the bilingual dictionary and the collection of texts to make a comparison of text pairs in a subsequent stage faster. A comparison

Proceedings of the Workshop on Multilingual Language Resources and Interoperability, pages 60–67,
Sydney, July 2006. ©2006 Association for Computational Linguistics

of a text pair is carried out simply by comparing two streams of integers without any dictionary or table lookup, in time linear in the sum of the two text sizes. With this method, we achieved 250,000 pairs/sec throughput on a single Xeon CPU (2.4GHz). The best F_1 score is 0.960, for a dataset which includes 200 true pairs out of 40,000 candidate pairs. Further comments on these numbers are given in Section 4.

In addition, to the best of our knowledge, this is the first reported experiment of extracitng Japanese–English parallel texts using a method solely based on their linguistic contents.

2 Related Work

There have been several attempts to collect parallel texts from the Web. We will mention two contrasting approaches among them.

2.1 BITS

Ma and Liberman collected English–German parallel webpages (Ma and Liberman, 1999). They began with a list of websites that belong to a domain accosiated with German–speaking areas and searched for parallel webpages in these sites. For each site, they downloaded a subset of the site to investigate what language it is written in, and then, downloaded all pages if it was proved to be English–German bilingual. For each pair of English and German document, they judged whether it is a mutual translation. They made a decision in the following manner. First, they searched a bilingual dictionary for all English–German word pairs in the text pair. If a word pair is found in the dictionary, it is recognized as an evidence of translation. Finally, they divided the number of recognized pairs by the sum of the length of the two texts and regard this value as a score of translationality. When this score is greater than a given threshold, the pair is judged as a mutual translation. They succeeded in creating about 63MB parallel corpus with 10 machines through 20 days.

The number of webpages is considered to have increased far more rapidly than the performance of computers in the past seven years. Therefore, we think it is important to reduce the cost of calculation of a system.

2.2 STRAND

If we simply make a dicision for all pairs in a collection of texts, the calculation takes $\Omega(n^2)$ comparisons of text pairs where n is the number of documents in the collection. In fact, most researches utilize properties peculiar to certain parallel webpages to reduce the number of candidate pairs in advance. Resnik and Smith focused on the fact that a page pair tends to be a mutual translation when their URL strings meet a certain condition, and examined only page pairs which satisfy it (Resnik and Smith, 2003). A URL string sometimes contains a substring which indicates the language in which the page is written. For example, a webpage written in Japanese sometimes have a substring such as `j`, `jp`, `jpn`, `n`, `euc` or `sjis` in its URL. They regard a pair of pages as a candidate when their URLs match completely after removing such language-specific substrings and, only for these candidates, did they make a detailed comparison with bilingual dictionary. They were successful in collecting 2190 parallel pairs from 8294 candidates. However, this URL condition seems so strict for the purpose that they found 8294 candidate pairs from as much as 20 Tera bytes of webpages.

3 Proposed Method

3.1 Problem settings

There are several evaluation criteria for parallel text mining algorithms. They include accuracy, execution speed, and generality. We say an algorithm is general when it can be applied to texts of any format, not only to webpages with associated information specific to webpages (e.g., URLs and tags). In this paper, we focus on developing a fast and general algorithm for determining if a pair of texts is parallel.

In general, there are two complementary ways to improve the speed of parallel text mining. One is to reduce the number of "candidate pairs" to be compared. The other is to make a single comparison of two texts faster. An example of the former is Resnik and Smith's URL matching method, which is able to mine parallel texts from a very large corpora of Tera bytes. However, this approach is very specific to the Web and, even if we restrict our interest to webpages, there may be a significant number of parallel pages whose URLs do not match the prescribed pattern and therefore are filtered out. Our method is in the latter category, and is generally applicable to texts of any format. The approach depends only on the linguistic content of texts. Reducing the number of

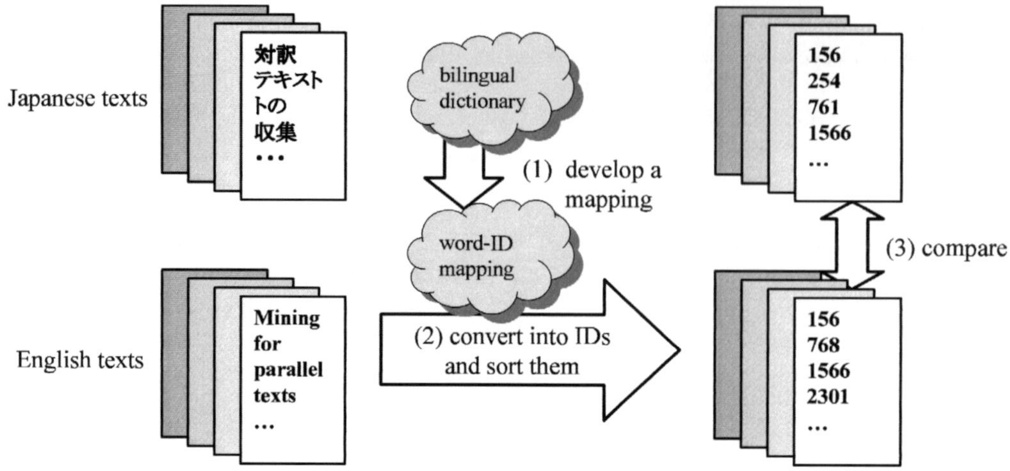

Figure 1: Outline of the method

comparisons while maintaining the generality will be one of our future works.

The outline of the method is as follows. First we preprocess a bilingual dictionary and build a mapping from words to integers, which we call "semantic ID." Texts are then preprocessed, converting each word to its corresponding semantic ID plus its position of the occurrence. Then we compare all pairs of texts, using their converted representations (Figure 1). Comparing a pair of texts is fast because it is performed in time linear in the length of the texts and does not need any table lookup or string manipulation.

3.2 Preprocessing a bilingual dictionary

We take only nouns into account in our algorithm. For the language pair of English and Japanese, a correspondence of parts of speech of a word and its translation is not so clear and may make the problem more difficult. A result was actually worse when every open-class word was considered than when only nouns were.

The first stage of the method is to assign an integer called semantic ID to every word (in both languages) that appears in a bilingual dictionary. The goal is to assign the same ID to a pair of words that are translations of each other. In an ideal situation where each word of one language corresponds one-to-one with a word of the other language, all you need to do is to assign differnt IDs to every translational relationship between two words. The main purpose of this conversion is to make a comparison of two texts in a subsequent stage faster.

However, it's not exactly that simple. A word very often has more than one words as its translation so the naive method described above is not directly applicable. We devised an approximate solution to address this complexity. We build a bigraph whose nodes are words in the dictionary and edges translational relationships between them. This graph consists of many small connected components, each representing a group of words that are expected to have similar meanings. We then make a mapping from a word to its semantic ID. Two words are considered translations of each other when they have the same semantic ID.

This method causes a side-effect of connecting two words not directly related in the dictionary. It has both good and bad effects. A good effect is that it may connect two words that do not explicitly appear as translations in the dictionary, but are used as translations in practice (see section 4.3). In other words, new translational word pairs are detected. A bad effect, on the other hand, is that it potentially connects many words that do not share meanings at all. Figure 2 shows an actual example of such an undesirable component observed in our experiment. You can go from *fruit* to *army* through several hops and these words are treated as identical entity in subsequent steps of our technique. Futhermore, in the most extreme case, a very large connected component can be created. Table 1 shows the statistics of the component sizes for the English-Japanese dictionary we have used in our experiment (EDR Electronic Dictionary).

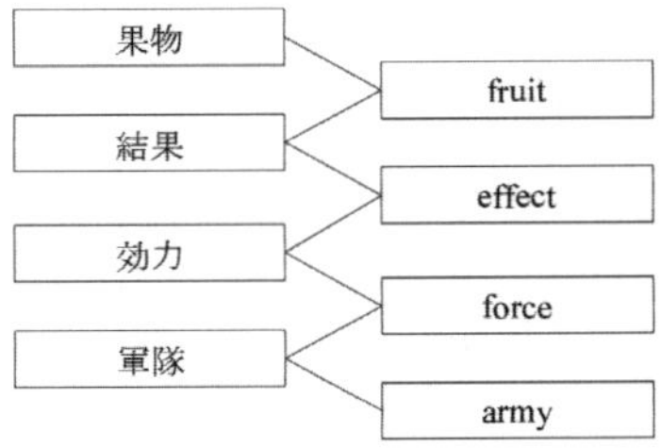

Figure 2: Example of a undesirable graph

Most components are fairly small (< 10 words). The largest connected component, however, consisted of 3563 nodes out of the total 28001 nodes in the entire graph and 3943 edges out of 19413. As we will see in the next section, this had a devastating effect on the quality of judgement so we clearly need a method that circumvents the situation. One possibility is to simply drop very large components. Another is to divide the graph into small components. We have tried both approaches.

Table 1: Statistics of the component sizes

# of nodes	# of components
2	6629
3	1498
4	463
5	212
6	125
7	69
8	44
9	32
10~	106

For partitioning graphs, we used a very simple greedy method. Even though a more complex method may be possible that takes advantages of linguistic insights, this work uses a very simple partitioning method that only looks at the graph structure in this work. A graph is partitioned into two parts having an equal number of nodes and a partition is recursively performed until each part becomes smaller than a given threshold. The threshold is chosen so that it yields the best result for a training set and then applied to a test data. For each bisection, we begin with a random partition and improves it by a local greedy search. Given the current partition, it seeks a pair of nodes which, if swapped, maximumly reduces the number of edges crossing the two parts. Ties are broken arbitrarily when there are many such pairs. If no single swap reduces the number of edges across parts, we simply stop (i.e., local search). A semantic ID is then given to each part.

This process would lose connections between words that are originally translations in the dictionary but are separated by the partitioning. We will describe a method to partially recover this loss in the end of the next section, after describing how texts are preprocessed.

3.3 Preprocessing texts

Each text (document) is preprocessed as follows. Texts are segmented into words and tagged with a part-of-speech. Inflection problems are addressed with lemmatization. Each word is converted into the pair (*nid*, *pos*), where *nid* is the semantic ID of the partition containing the word and *pos* its position of occurrence. The position is normalized and represented as a floating point number between 0.0 and 1.0. Any word which does not appear in the dictionary is simply ignored. The position is used to judge if words having an equal ID occur in similar positions in both texts, so they suggest a translation.

After converting each word, all (*nid*, *pos*) pairs are sorted first by their semantic IDs breaking ties with positions. This sorting takes $O(n \log n)$ time for a document of n words. This preprocessing needs to be performed only once for each document.

We recover the connections between word pairs separated by the partitioning in the following manner. Suppose words J and E are translations of each other in the dictionary, J is in a partition whose semantic ID is x and E in another partition whose semantic ID is y. In this case, we translate J into two elements x and y. This result is as if two separate words, one in component x and another in y, appeared in the original text, so it may potentially have an undesirable side-effect on the quality of judgement. It is therefore important to keep the number of such pairs reasonably small. We experimented with both cases, one in which we recover separate connections and the other in which we don't.

3.4 Comparing document pairs

We judge if a text pair is likely to be a translation by comparing two sequences obtained by the preprocessing. We count the number of word pairs that have an equal semantic ID and whose positions are within a distance threshold. The best threshold is chosen to yield the best result for a training set and then applied to test set. This process takes time linear in the length of texts since the sequences are sorted. First, we set cursors at the first element of each of the two sequences. When the semantic IDs of the elements under the cursors are equal and the difference between their positions is within a threshold, we count them as an evidence of translationality and move both cursors forward. Otherwise, the cursor on the element which is less according to the sorting criteria is moved forward. In this step, we do not perform any further search to determine if original words of the elements were related directly in the bilingual dictionary giving preference to speed over accuracy. We repeat this operation until any of the cursors reaches the end of the sequence. Finally, we divide the number of matching elements by the sum of the lengths of the two documents. We define this value as "tscore," which stands for translational score. At least one cursor moves after each comparison, so this algorithm finishes in time linear in the length of the texts.

4 Experiments

4.1 Preparation

To evaluate our method, we used The EDR Electronic Dictionary[1] for a bilingual dictionary and Fry's Japanese-English parallel web corpus (Fry, 2005) for sample data. In this experiment, we considered only nouns (see section 3.2) and got a graph which consists of 28001 nodes, 19413 edges and 9178 connected components of which the largest has 3563 nodes and 3943 edges. Large components including it need to be partitioned.

We conducted partitioning with differnt thresholds and developed various word–ID mappings. For each mapping, we made several variations in two respect. One is whether cut connections are recovered or not. The other is whether and how many numerals, which can be easily utilized to boost the vocaburary of the dictionary, are added to a bilingual dictionary.

The parallel corpus we used had been collected by Fry from four news sites. Most texts in the corpus are news report on computer technology and the rest is on various fields of science. A single document is typically 1,000–6,000 bytes. He detected parallel texts based only on HTML tags and link structures, which depend on websites, without looking at textual content, so there are many false pairs in his corpus. Therefore, to evaluate our method precisely, we used only 400 true parallel pairs that are randomly selected and checked by human inspection. We divided them evenly and randomly into two parts and use one half for a training set and the other for a test set. In experiments described in section 4.4 and 4.5, we used other portion of the corpus to scale experiments.

For tokenization and pos-tagging, we used MeCab[2] to Japanese texts and SS Tagger[3] to English texts. Because SS Tagger doesn't act as lemmatizer, we used `morphstr()` function in WordNet library[4].

4.2 Effect of large components and a partitioning

Figure 3 shows the results of experiments on several conditions. There are three groups of bars; (A) treat every connected component equally regardless of its size, (B) simply drop the largest component and (C) divide large components into smaller parts. In each group, the upper bar corresponds to the case the algorithm works without a distance threshold and the lower with it (0.2). The figures attached to each bar are the $\max F_1$ score, which is a popular measure to evaluate a classification algorithm, and indicate how accurately a method is able to detect 200 true text pairs from the test set of 40,000 pairs. We didn't recover word connections broken in the partitioning step and didn't add any numerals to the vocabrary of the bilingual dictionary this time.

The significant difference between (A) and (B) clearly shows the devastating effect of large components. The difference between (B) and (C) shows that the accurary can be further improved if large components are partitioned into small ones in order to utilize as much information as possible. In addtion, the accuracy consistently improves by using the distance threshold.

Next, we determined the best word–ID mapping

[1]EDR Electronic Dictionary.
http://www2.nict.go.jp/kk/e416/EDR/

[2]MeCab: Yet Another Part-of-Speech and Morphological Analyzer.
http://mecab.sourceforge.jp/

[3]SS Tagger - a part-of-speech tagger for English.
http://www-tsujii.is.s.u-tokyo.ac.jp/~tsuruoka/postagger/

[4]WordNet - a lexical database for the English language.
http://wordnet.princeton.edu/

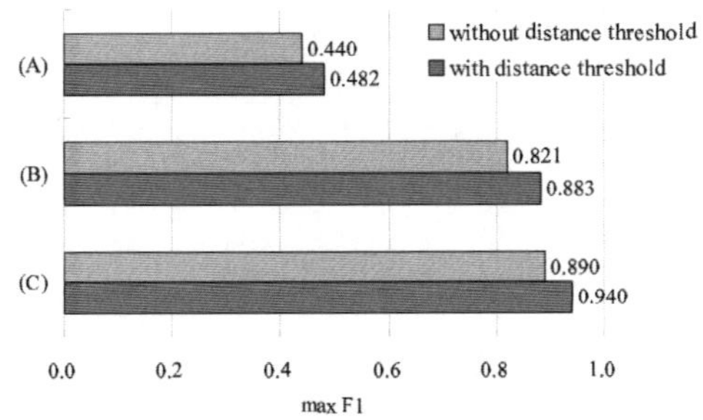

Figure 3: Effect of the graph partitioning

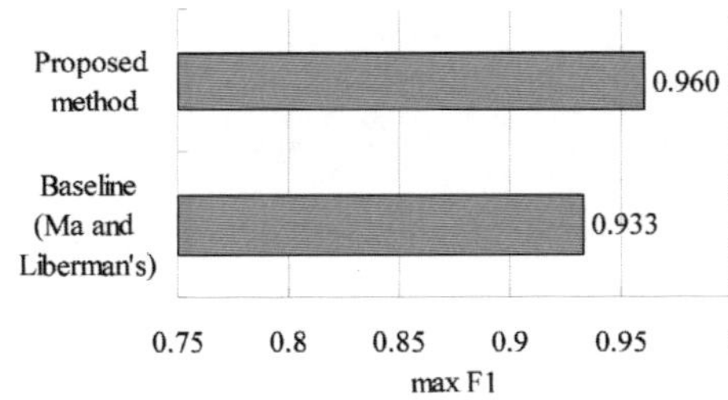

Figure 4: The two word-matching policy

and distance threshold and tested its performance through a 2–fold cross validation. The best mapping among those was the one which

- divides a component recursively until the number of nodes of each language becomes no more than 30,
- does not recover connections that are cut in the partitioning, and
- adds numerals from 0 to 999.

The best distance threshold was 0.2, and tscore threshold 0.102. We tested this rule and thresholds on the test set. The result was $F_1 = 0.960$.

4.3 Effect of false translation pairs

Our method of matching words differs from Ma and Liberman's one. While they only count word pairs that directly appear in a bilingual dictionary, we identify all words having the same semantic ID. Potential merits and drawbacks to accuracy have been described in the section 3.2. We compared the accuracy of the two algorithms to investigate the effect of our approximate matching. To this end, we implemented Ma and Liberman's method with all other conditions and input data being equal to the one in the last section. We got $\max F_1 = 0.933$ as a result, which is slightly worse than the figure reported in their paper. Though it is difficult to conclude where the difference stems from, there are several factors worth pointing out. First, our experiment is done for English-Japanese, while Ma and Liberman's experiment for English-German, which are more similar than English and Japanese are. Second, their data set contains much more true pairs (240 out of 300) than our data set does (200 out of 40,000).

This number is also worse than that of our experiment (Figure 4). This shows that, at least in the experiment, our approach of identifying more pairs than the original dictionary causes more good effects than bad in total. We looked at word pairs which are not matched in Ma and Liberman's method but in ours. While most of the pairs can be hardly considered as a strict translation, some of them are pairs practically used as translations. Examples of such pairs are shown in Figure 5.

English word	Japanese word
issue	課題
competition	コンテスト
dicision	決意
sum	総額
benefit	利点
phone	電話器
device	発明
client	買手

Figure 5: Word pairs not in the dictionary

4.4 Execution Speed

We have argued that the execution speed is a major advantage of our method. We achieved 250,000 pairs/sec throughput on single Xeon (2.4GHz) processor. It's difficult to make a fair comparison of the execution speed because Ma and Liberman's paper does not describe enough details about their experimants other than processing 3145 websites with 10 sparc stations for 10 days. Just for a rough estimate, we introduce some bold assumptions. Say, there were a thousand pages for each language in a website or, in other words, a million page pairs, and the performance of processors has grown by 32 times in the past seven years, our method works more than 40 times faster than Ma and Liberman's one. This difference seems

English text	Japanese text
The results of two new studies may completely transform the way scientists worldwide approach the field of stem **cell** research. Scientists have long believed that stem **cells** -- derived from blood, bone marrow or embryos -- are capable of repairing damaged tissue by taking on the identity of that organ's **cells**, a phenomenon known as differentiation. But the new studies show that in the diseased livers of mice, stem **cells** didn't differentiate. Instead, they fused with the injured liver **cells** to perform the necessary repairs. The finding is controversial, especially among stem **cell** researchers who have devoted a lot of energy to uncovering a way to induce the **cells** to change identity. (snip)	動物の成体がもつ特定の組織の幹**細胞**にも、その組織以外のさまざまな種類の**細胞**を作り出す力があることを示す新しい証拠が、20日(米国時間)報告された。疾病治療への応用が期待される。 一般に、万能性に近いこのような多能性は、幹**細胞**の分化が進む前の胚の段階における胚性幹**細胞**(ES**細胞**)にしか存在しないと考えられているが、今回の研究の結果は、成体の幹**細胞**が胚性幹**細胞**に代わる有用な選択肢になり得ることを示唆している。ヒトの胚性幹**細胞**の利用については、その採取の過程で胚を犠牲にすることが避けられないため、是非を巡って議論が巻き起こっている。 病気の治療を想定した場合、患者本人から何らかの幹**細胞**を採取し、たとえば糖尿病患者の場合ならインシュリン生成**細胞**というように、患者が必要としているタイプの**細胞**を作り出し、それを再び患者の体内に戻すことが可能だとされている。 (以下略)

Figure 6: A example of false–positive text pairs

to be caused by a difference of the complexity between the two algorithms. To the extent written in their paper, Ma and Liberman calculated a score of translationality by enumerating all combinations of two words within a distance threshold and search a bilingual dictionary for each combination of words. This algorithm takes $\Omega(n^2)$ time where n is the length of a text, while our method takes $O(n)$ time. In addition, our method doesn't need any string manipulation in the comparison step.

4.5 Analysis of miss detections

We analyzed text pairs for which judgements differ between Fry's and ours.

Among pairs Fry determined as a translation, we examined the 10 pairs ranked highest in our algorithm. Two of them are in fact translations, which were not detected by Fry's method without any linguistic information. The rest eight pairs are not translations. Three of the eight pairs are about bioscience, and a word "cell" occurred many time (Figure 6). When words with an identical semantic ID appear repeatedly in two texts being compared, their distances are likely to be within a distance threshold and the pair gets unreasonably high tscore. Therefore, if we take the number of each semantic ID in a text into account, we might be able to improve the accuracy.

We performed the same examination on the 10 pairs ranked lowest among those Fry determined not to be a translation. But no interesting feature could be found at the moment.

5 Summary and Future Work

In this paper, we proposed a fast and accurate method for detecting parallel texts from a collection. This method consists of major three parts; preprocess a bilingual dictionary into word–ID conversion rule, convert texts into ID sequences, compare sequences. With this method, we achieved 250,000 pairs/sec on a single CPU and best F_1 score of 0.960. In addition, this method utilizes only linguistic information of a textual content so that it is generally applicable. This means it can detect parallel documents in any format. Furthermore, our method is independent on languages in essence. It can be applied to any pair of languages if a bilingual dictionary between the languages are available (a general language dictionary suffices.)

Our future study will include improving both accuracy and speed while retaining the generaility. For accuracy, as we described in Section 4.5, tscore tends to increase when an identical semantic ID appears many times in a text. We might be able to deal with this problem by taking into account the probability that the distance between words is within a threshold. Large connected components were partitioned by a very simple method at the present work. More involved partitioning methods may improve the accuracy of the judgement. For speed, reducing the number of comparisons is the most important issue that needs be addressed.

References

Peter F. Brown, John Cocke, Stephen A. Della Pietra, Vincent J. Della Pietra, Fredrick Jelinek, John D. Lafferty, Robert L. Mercer, and Paul S. Roossin. 1990. A statistical approach to machine translation. *Comput. Linguist.*, 16(2):79–85.

Jiang Chen and Jian-Yun Nie. 2000. Automatic construction of parallel english-chinese corpus for cross-language information retrieval. In *Proceedings of the sixth conference on Applied natural language processing*, pages 21–28, San Francisco, CA, USA. Morgan Kaufmann Publishers Inc.

John Fry. 2005. Assembling a parallel corpus from RSS news feeds. In *Workshop on Example-Based Machine Translation, MT Summit X, Phuket, Thailand*, September.

Xiaoyi Ma and Mark Liberman. 1999. BITS: A method for bilingual text search over the web. In *Machine Translation Summit VII*, September.

David Nadeau and George Foster. 2004. Real-time identification of parallel texts from bilingual newsfeed. In *Computational Linguistic in the North-East (CLiNE 2004)*, pages 21–28.

Makoto Nagao, editor. 1996. *Natural Language Processing*. Number 15 in Iwanami Software Science. Iwanami Shoten. In Japanese.

Philip Resnik and Noah A. Smith. 2003. The web as a parallel corpus. *Comput. Linguist.*, 29(3):349–380.

C. C. Yang and K. W. Li. 2002. Mining English/Chinese parallel documents from the World Wide Web. In *Proceedings of the International World Wide Web Conference*, Honolulu, Hawaii, May.

Evaluation of the Bible as a Resource for Cross-Language Information Retrieval

Peter A. Chew **Steve J. Verzi** **Travis L. Bauer** **Jonathan T. McClain**
Sandia National Laboratories
P. O. Box 5800
Albuquerque, NM 87185, USA
{pchew,sjverzi,tlbauer,jtmccl}@sandia.gov

Abstract

An area of recent interest in cross-language information retrieval (CLIR) is the question of which parallel corpora might be best suited to tasks in CLIR, or even to what extent parallel corpora can be obtained or are necessary. One proposal, which in our opinion has been somewhat overlooked, is that the Bible holds a unique value as a multilingual corpus, being (among other things) widely available in a broad range of languages and having a high coverage of modern-day vocabulary. In this paper, we test empirically whether this claim is justified through a series of validation tests on various information retrieval tasks. Our results appear to indicate that our methodology may significantly outperform others recently proposed.

1 Introduction

This paper describes an empirical evaluation of the Bible as a resource for cross-language information retrieval (CLIR). The paper is organized as follows: section 2 describes the background to this project and explains our need for CLIR. Section 3 sets out the various alternatives available (as far as multilingual corpora are concerned) for the type of textual CLIR which we want to perform, and details in qualitative terms why the Bible would appear to be a good candidate. In section 4, we outline the mechanics behind the 'Rosetta-Stone' type method we use for cross-language comparison. The manner in which both this method, and the reliability of using the Bible as the basis for cross-language comparison, are validated is outlined in section 5, together with the results of our tests. Finally, we conclude on and discuss these results in section 6.

2 Background

This paper describes a project which is part of a larger, ongoing, undertaking, the goal of which is to harvest a representative sample of material from the internet and determine, on a very broad scale, the answers to such questions as:

- what ideas in the global public discourse enjoy most currency;
- how the popularity of ideas changes over time.

Ideas are, of course, expressed in words; or, to put it another way, a document's vocabulary is likely to reveal something about the author's ideology (Lakoff, 2002). In view of this, and since ultimately we are interested in clustering the documents harvested from the internet by their ideology (and we understand 'ideology' in the broadest possible sense), we approach the problem as a textual information retrieval (IR) task.

There is another level of complexity to the problem, however. The language of the internet is not, of course, confined to English; on the contrary, the representation of other languages is probably increasing (Hill and Hughes, 1998; Nunberg, 2000). Thus, for our results to be representative, we require a way to compare documents in one language to those in potentially any other language. Essentially, we would like to answer the question of how ideologically aligned two documents are, regardless of their respective languages. In cross-language IR, this must be approached by the use of a parallel multilingual corpus, or at least some kind of appropriate training material available in multiple languages.

3 Parallel multilingual corpora: available alternatives

One collection of multilingual corpora gathered with a specific view towards CLIR has been de-

Proceedings of the Workshop on Multilingual Language Resources and Interoperability, pages 68–74,
Sydney, July 2006.

veloped by the Cross-Language Evaluation Forum (CLEF); see, for example, Gonzalo (2001). This collection, and its most recent revision (at the CLEF website, www.clef-campaign.org), are based on news documents or governmental communications. Use of such corpora is widespread in much recent CLIR work; one such example is Nie, Simard, Isabelle and Durand (1999), which uses the Hansard corpus, parallel French-English texts of eight years of the Canadian parliamentary proceedings, to train a CLIR model.

It should be noted that the stated objective of CLEF is to 'develop and maintain an infrastructure for the testing and evaluation of information retrieval systems operating on European languages' (Peters 2001:1). Indeed, there is good reason for this: CLEF is an activity under the auspices of the European Commission. Likewise, the Canadian Hansard corpus covers only English and French, the most widespread languages of Canada. It is to be expected that governmental institutions would have most interest in promoting resources and research in the languages falling most within their respective domains.

But in many ways, not least for the computational linguistics community, nor for anyone interested in understanding trends in global opinion, this represents an inherent limitation. Since many of the languages of interest for our project are not European – Arabic is a good example – resources such as the CLEF collection will be insufficient by themselves. The output of global news organizations is a more promising avenue, because many such organizations make an effort to provide translations in a wide variety of languages. For example, the BBC news website (http://news.bbc.co.uk/) provides translations in 34 languages, as follows:

> Albanian, Arabic, Azeri, Bengali, Burmese, Chinese, Czech, English, French, Hausa, Hindi, Indonesian, Kinyarwanda, Kirundi, Kyrgyz, Macedonian, Nepali, Pashto, Persian, Portuguese, Romanian, Russian, Serbian, Sinhala, Slovene, Somali, Spanish, Swahili, Tamil, Turkish, Ukrainian, Urdu, Uzbek, Vietnamese

However, there is usually no assurance that a news article in one language will be translated into any, let alone all, of the other languages.

In view of this, even more promising still as a parallel corpus for our purposes is the Bible. Resnik, Olsen and Diab (1999) elaborate on some of the reasons for this: it is the world's most translated book, with translations in over 2,100 languages (often, multiple translations per language) and easy availability, often in electronic form and in the public domain; it covers a variety of literary styles including narrative, poetry, and correspondence; great care is taken over the translations; it has a standard structure which allows parallel alignment on a verse-by-verse basis; and, perhaps surprisingly, its vocabulary appears to have a high rate of coverage (as much as 85%) of modern-day language. Resnik, Olsen and Diab note that the Bible is small compared to many corpora currently used in computational linguistics research, but still falls within the range of acceptability based on the fact that other corpora of similar size are used; and as previously noted, the breadth of languages covered is simply not available elsewhere. This in itself makes the Bible attractive to us as a resource for our CLIR task. It is an open question whether, because of the Bible's content, relatively small size, or some other attribute, it can successfully be used for the type of CLIR we envisage. The rest of this paper describes our attempt to establish a definitive answer to this question.

4 Methods for Cross-Language Comparison

All of the work described in this section was implemented using the Sandia Text Analysis Extensible Library (STANLEY). STANLEY allows for information retrieval based on a standard vector model (Baeza-Yates and Ribeiro-Neto, 1999: 27-30) with term weighting based on log entropy. Previous work (Bauer et al 2005) has shown that the precision-recall curve for STANLEY is better than many other published algorithms; Dumais (1991) finds specifically that the precision-recall curve for information retrieval based on log-entropy weighting compares favorably to that for other weighting schemes. Two distinct methods for cross-language comparison are described in this section, and these are as follows.

The first method (Method 1) involves creating a separate textual model for each 'minimal unit' of each translation of the Bible. A 'minimal unit' could be as small as a verse (e.g. Genesis 1:1), but it could be a group of verses (e.g. Genesis 1:1-10); the key is that alignment is possible because of the chapter-and-verse structure of the Bible, and that whatever grouping is used should be the same in each translation. Thus, for each language λ we end up with a set of models ($m_{1,\lambda}$, $m_{2,\lambda}$, … $m_{n,\lambda}$). If the Bible is used as the parallel corpus and the 'minimal unit' is the verse, then n = 31,102 (the number of verses in the Bible).

Let us suppose now that we wish to compare document d_i with document d_j, and that we happen to know that d_i is in English and d_j is in Russian. In order to assess to what extent d_i and d_j are 'about' the same thing, we treat the text of each document as a query against all of the models in its respective language. So, d_i is evaluated against $m_{1,English}$, $m_{2,English}$, …, $m_{n,English}$ to give $sim_{i,1}$, $sim_{i,2}$, …, $sim_{i,n}$, where $sim_{x,y}$ (a value between 0 and 1) represents the similarity of document d_x in language λ to model m_n in language λ, based on the cosine of the angle between the vector for d_x and the vector for m_n. Similar evaluations are performed for d_j against the set of models in Russian. Now, each set of n results for a particular document can itself be thought of an n-dimensional vector. Thus, d_i is associated with ($sim_{i,1}$, $sim_{i,2}$, …, $sim_{i,n}$) and d_j with ($sim_{j,1}$, $sim_{j,2}$, …, $sim_{j,n}$). To quantify the similarity between d_i and d_j, we now compute the cosine between these two vectors to yield a single measure, also a value between 0 and 1. In effect, we have used the multilingual corpus – the Bible, in this case – in 'Rosetta-Stone' fashion to bridge the language gap between d_i and d_j. Method 1 is summarized graphically in Figure 1, for two hypothetical documents.

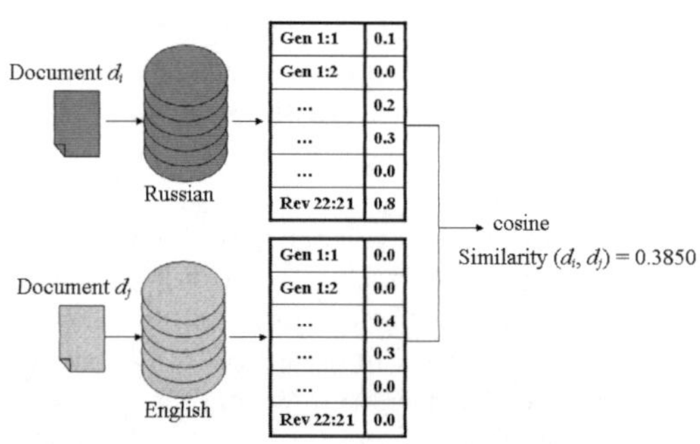

Figure 1: Method 1 for cross-language comparison

The second method of comparison (Method 2) is quite similar. This time, however, instead of building one set of textual models for each translation in language λ ($m_{1,\lambda}$, $m_{2,\lambda}$, … $m_{n,\lambda}$), we build a *single* set of textual models for *all* translations, with each language represented at least once (m_1, m_2, … m_n). Thus, m_1 might represent a model based on the concatenation of Genesis 1:1 in English, Russian, Arabic, and so on. In a fashion similar to that of Method 1, each incoming document d_i is evaluated as a query against m_1, m_2, …, m_n, to give an n-dimensional vector where each cell is a value between 0 and 1. Method 2 is summarized graphically in Figure 2, for just English and Russian.

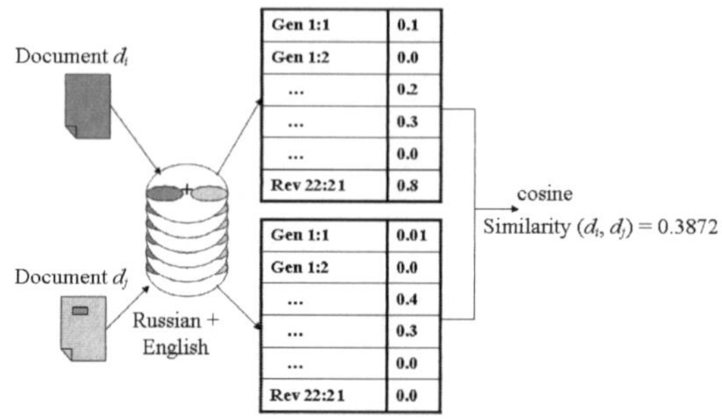

Figure 2: Method 2 for cross-language comparison

There are at least two features of Method 2 which make it attractive, from a linguist's point of view, for CLIR. The first is that it allows for the possibility that a single input document may be multilingual. In Figure 2, document d_j is represented by an symbol with a mainly light-colored background, but with a small dark-colored section. This is intended to represent a document with mainly English content, but some small subsection in Russian. Under Method 1, in which d_j is compared to an English-language model, the Russian content would have been effectively ignored, but under Method 2 this is no longer the case. Accordingly, the hypothetical similarity measure for the first 'minimal unit' has changed very slightly, as has the overall measure of similarity between document d_i and d_j.

The second linguistic attraction of Method 2 is that it is not necessary to know a priori the language of d_i or d_j, providing that the language is one of those for which we have textual data in the model set. Since, as already stated, the Bible covers over 2,100 languages, this should not be a significant theoretical impediment.

The theoretical advantages of Method 1 have principally to do with the ease of technical implementation. New model sets for additional languages can be easily added as they become available, whereas under Method 2 the entire model set must be rebuilt (statistics recomputed, etc.) each time a new language is added.

5 Validation of the Bible as a resource for CLIR

In previous sections, we have rehearsed some of the qualitative arguments for our choice of the

Bible as the basis for CLIR. In this section, we consider how this choice may be validated empirically. We would like to know how reliable the cross-language comparison methods outlined in the previous section are at identifying documents in different languages but which happen to be similar in content. This reliability will be in part a function of the particular text analysis model we employ, but it will also be a function of our choice of parallel text used to train the model. The Bible has some undeniable qualitative advantages for our purposes, but are the CLIR results based on it satisfactory in practice? Three tests are described in this section; the aim of these is to provide an answer to this question.

5.1 Preliminary analysis

In order to obtain a preliminary idea of whether this method was likely to work, we populated the entire matrix of similarity measures, verse by verse, for each language pair. There are 31,102 verses in the Bible (allowing for some variation in versification between different translations, which we carefully controlled for by adopting a common versification schema). Thus, this step involved building a 31,102 by 31,102 matrix for each language pair, in which the cell in row *m* and column *n* contains a number between 0 and 1 representing the similarity of verse *m* in one language to verse *n* in the other language. If use of the Bible for CLIR is a sound approach, we would expect to see the highest similarity measures in what we will call the matrix's diagonal values – the values occurring down the diagonal of the matrix from top-left to bottom-right – meaning that verse *n* in one language is most similar to verse *n* in the other, for all *n*.

Here, we would simply like to note an incidental finding. We found that for certain language pairs, the diagonal values were significantly higher than for other language pairs, as shown in Table 1.

Language pair	Mean similarity, verse by verse
English-Russian	0.3728
English-Spanish	0.5421
English-French	0.5508
Spanish-French	0.5691

Table 1. Mean similarities by language pair

One hypothesis we have is that the lower overall similarity for English-Russian is at least partly due to the fact that Russian is a much more highly inflected language then any of English, French, or Spanish. That many verses containing non-dictionary forms are the ones that score the highest for similarity, and many of those that do not score lowest, appears to confirm this. However, there appear to be other factors at play as well, since many of the highest-scoring verses contain proper names or other infrequently occurring lexical items (examples are Esther 9:9: 'and Parmashta, and Arisai, and Aridai, and Vaizatha', and Exodus 37:19: 'three cups made like almond-blossoms in one branch, a bud and a flower, and three cups made like almond-blossoms in the other branch, a bud and a flower: so for the six branches going out of the lampstand'). A third possibility, consistent with the first, is that Table 1 actually reflects more general measures of similarity between languages, the Western European languages (for example) all being more closely related to Latin than their Slavic counterparts. At any rate, if our hypothesis about inflection being an important factor is correct, then this would seem to underline the importance of stemming for highly-inflected languages.

5.2 Simple validation

In this test, the CLIR algorithm is trained on the entire Bible, and validation is performed against available extra-Biblical multilingual corpora such as the FQS (2006) and RALI (2006) corpora. This test, together with the tests already described, should provide a reliable measure of how well our CLIR model will work when applied to our target domain (documents collected from the internet).

For this test, five abstracts in the FQS (2006) were selected. These abstracts are in both Spanish and English, and the five are listed in Table 2 below.

Eng. 1	Perspectives
Eng. 2	Public and Private Narratives
Eng. 3	Qualitative Research
Eng. 4	How Much Culture is Psychology Able to Deal With
Eng. 5	Conference Report
Sp. 1	Perspectivas
Sp. 2	Narrativas públicas y privadas
Sp. 3	Cuánta cultura es capaz de abordar la Psicología
Sp. 4	Investigación cualitativa
Sp. 5	Nota sobre la conferencia

Table 2. Documents selected for analysis

The results based on these five abstracts, where comparison was performed between Spanish and English and vice-versa, are as shown in Table 3. The results shown in Table 3 are the actual (raw) similarity values provided by our CLIR framework using the FQS corpus.

	Eng. 1	Eng. 2	Eng. 3	Eng. 4	Eng. 5
Sp. 1	0.6067	0.0430	0.0447	0.0821	0.1661
Sp. 2	0.0487	0.3969	0.0377	0.0346	0.0223
Sp. 3	0.1018	0.0956	0.0796	0.1887	0.1053
Sp. 4	0.0303	0.0502	0.0450	0.1013	0.0493
Sp. 5	0.0354	0.1314	0.0387	0.0425	0.1682

Table 3. Raw similarity values of Spanish and English documents from FQS corpus

In this table, 'Eng. 1', 'Sp. 1', etc., refer to the documents as listed in Table 2.

In four out of five cases, the CLIR engine correctly predicted which English document was related to which Spanish document, and in four out of five cases it also correctly predicted which Spanish document was related to which English document. We can relate these results to traditional IR measures such as precision-recall and mean average precision by using a query that returns the top-most similar document. Thus, our 'right' answer set as well as our CLIR answers will consist of a single document. For the FQS corpus, this represents a mean average precision (MAP) of 0.8 at a recall point of 1 (the first document recalled). The incorrect cases were Eng. 4, where Sp. 3 was predicted, and Sp. 3, where Eng. 4 was predicted. (By way of possible explanation, both these two documents included the keywords 'qualitative research' with the abstract.) Furthermore, in most of the cases where the prediction was correct, there is a clear margin between the score for the correct choice and the scores for the incorrect choices. This leads us to believe that our general approach to CLIR is at very least promising.

5.3 Validation on a larger test set

To address the question of whether the CLIR approach performs as well on larger test sets, where the possibility of an incorrect prediction is greater simply because there are more documents to select from, we trained the CLIR engine on the Bible and validated it against the 114 suras of the Quran, performing a four-by-four-way test using the original Arabic (AR) text plus English (EN), Russian (RU) and Spanish (ES) translations. The MAP at a recall point of 1 is shown for each language pair in Table 4.

		Language of predicted document			
		AR	**EN**	**RU**	**ES**
Language of input	**AR**	1.0000	0.2193	0.2281	0.2105
	EN	0.2632	1.0000	0.3333	0.5263
	RU	0.2719	0.3860	1.0000	0.4386
	ES	0.2105	0.4912	0.4035	1.0000

Table 4. Results based on Quran test

This table shows, for example, that for 52.63% (or 60) of the 114 English documents used as input, the correct Spanish document was retrieved first. As with the results in the previous section, we can relate these results to MAP at a recall of 1. If we were to consider more than just the top-most similar document in our CLIR output, we would expect the chance of seeing the correct document to increase. However, since in this experiment the number of relevant documents can never exceed 1, the precision will be diluted as more documents are retrieved (except at the point when the one correct document is retrieved). The values shown in the table are, of course, greater by a couple of orders of magnitude than that expected of random retrieval, of 0.0088 (1/114). Our methodology appears significantly to outperform that proposed by McNamee and Mayfield (2004), who report an MAP of 0.3539, and a precision of 0.4520 at a recall level of 10, for English-to-Spanish CLIR based on 5-gram tokenization. (We have not yet been able to compare our results to McNamee and Mayfield's using the same corpora that they use, but we intend to do this later. We do not expect our results to differ significantly from those we report above.) Perhaps not surprisingly, our results appear to be better for more closely-related languages, with pairs including Arabic being consistently those with the lowest average predictive precision across all suras.

6 Discussion

In this paper, we have presented a non-language-specific framework for cross-language information retrieval which appears promising at least for our purposes, and potentially for many others. It has the advantages of being easily extensible, and, with the results we have presented, it is empirically benchmarked. It is extensible in two dimensions; first, by language (substantially any human language which might be represented on the internet can be covered, and the cost of adding resources for each additional language is relatively small), secondly, by extending the training set with additional corpora, for available language pairs. Doubtless, also, the methodology could be further tuned for better performance.

It is perhaps surprising that the Bible has not been more widely used as a multilingual corpus by the computational linguistics and information retrieval community. In fact, it usually appears to be assumed by researchers that parallel texts, particularly those which have been as carefully translated as the Bible and are easy to align, are scarce and hard to come by (for two examples, see McNamee and Mayfield 2004 and Munteanu and Marcu 2006). The reason for the Bible being ignored may be the often unspoken assumption that the domain of the Bible is too limited (being a religious document) or that its content is too archaic. Yet, the truth is that much of the Bible's content has to do with enduring human concerns (life, death, war, love, etc.), and if the language is archaic, that may have more a matter of translation style than of content.

There are a number of future research directions in computational linguistics we would like to pursue, besides those which may be of interest in other disciplines. The first is to use this framework to evaluate the relative faithfulness of different translations. For example, we would expect to see similar statistical relationships within the model for a translation of the Bible as are seen in its original languages (Hebrew and Greek). Statistical comparisons could thus be used as the basis for evaluating a translation's faithfulness to the original. Such an analysis could be of theological, as well as linguistic, interest.

Secondly, we would like to examine whether the model's performance can be improved by introducing more sophisticated morphological analysis, so that the units of analysis are morphemes instead of words, or possibly morphemes as well as words.

Third, we intend to investigate further which of the two methods outlined in section 4 performs better in cross-language comparison, particularly when the language of the source document is unknown. In particular, we are interested in the extent to which homographic cognates across languages (e.g. French *coin* 'corner' versus English *coin*), may affect the performance of the CLIR engine.

Acknowledgement

Sandia is a multiprogram laboratory operated by Sandia Corporation, a Lockheed Martin Company, for the United States Department of Energy's National Nuclear Security Administration under contract DE-AC04-94AL85000.

References

Lars Asker. 2004. Building Resources: Experiences from Amharic Cross Language Information Retrieval. Paper presented at *Cross-Language Information Retrieval and Evaluation: Workshop of the Cross-Language Evaluation Forum, CLEF 2004.*

Ricardo Baeza-Yates and Berthier Ribeiro-Neto. 1999. *Modern Information Retrieval*. New York: ACM Press.

Travis Bauer, Steve Verzi, and Justin Basilico. 2005. Automated Context Modeling through Text Analysis. Paper presented at *Cognitive Systems: Human Cognitive Models in System Design*.

Susan Dumais. 1991. Improving the Retrieval of Information from External Sources. *Behavior Research Methods, Instruments, and Computers* 23(2):229-236.

Forum: Qualitative Social research (FQS). 2006. *Published Conference Reports*. (Conference reports available on-line in multiple languages.) Accessed at http://www.qualitative-research.net/fqs/conferences/conferences-pub-e.htm on February 22, 2006.

Julio Gonzalo. 2001. Language Resources in Cross-Language Text Retrieval: a CLEF Perspective. In Carol Peters (ed.). *Cross-Language Information Retrieval and Evaluation: Workshop of the Cross-Language Evaluation Forum, CLEF 2000*: 36-47. Berlin: Springer-Verlag.

George Lakoff. 2002. *Moral politics : how liberals and conservatives think*. Chicago : University of Chicago Press.

Paul McNamee and James Mayfield. 2004. Character *N*-Gram Tokenization for European Language Text Retrieval. *Information Retrieval* 7: 73-97.

Dragos Munteanu and Daniel Marcu. 2006. Improving Machine Translation Performance by Exploiting Non-Parallel Corpora. *Computational Linguistics* 31(4):477-504.

Geoffrey Nunberg. 2000. Will the Internet Always Speak English? *The American Prospect* 11(10).

Carol Peters (ed.). 2001. *Cross-Language Information Retrieval and Evaluation: Workshop of the Cross-Language Evaluation Forum, CLEF 2000*. Berlin: Springer-Verlag.

Recherche appliquée en linguistique informatique (RALI). 2006. *Corpus aligné bilingue anglais-français*. Accessed at http://rali.iro.umontreal.ca/ on February 22, 2006.

Philip Resnik, Mari Broman Olsen, and Mona Diab. 1999. The Bible as a Parallel Corpus: Annotating the "Book of 2000 Tongues". *Computers and the Humanities*, 33: 129-153.

Author Index

Association for Computational Linguistics
209 N. Eighth Street
Stroudsburg, Pennsylvania 18360